CATHERINE PHIPPS

EVERYDAY PRESSURE COOKING

Over 100 family favourites made fast and easy
in stovetop and electric pressure cookers

Photography by Andrew Hayes-Watkins

quadrille

INTRODUCTION

As you might imagine, people talk to me about pressure cooking a lot. I love this. I am delighted by the growing number of people who have overcome fears and/or scepticism and embraced pressure cooking. The phrase 'life-changing' is frequently used and I couldn't agree more. Pressure cooking is a way of cooking which bestows time and freedom and increases options. If you are one of the people who loves pressure cooking, you will already understand that it saves you time, fuel, money, water and – I often think – your sanity. If you want to cook at least some of your meals from scratch, it is the most useful piece of kitchen equipment you could buy.

And yet... One of the things people love to tell me is how often they use their pressure cooker: 'At least once/twice/three to four times a week!' At this point, my face falls and my mind immediately moves to wondering what they are cooking on all the other days of the week. The truth is, if you are using your pressure cooker to its full potential and you cook from scratch daily, you could be using it at least once a day, not once a week.

That is what this book is about. Within these pages I am hoping that you will find a collection of recipes which showcase the simplicity and versatility of pressure cooking, but also demonstrate how the cooker can be used day to day. Not just all the one-pot soups, stews, casseroles and curries for which we expect to use a pressure cooker but for the building blocks of everyday meals, for your side dishes, the cooked elements of your salads. I use mine constantly to make my life easier – whether it's for making a Thermos meal for my children to take to school every day, for reheating leftovers, or for cooking a pile of greens in less time than it takes for a full kettle to boil.

These recipes are a real mixture, but they all have one thing in common: they are all dishes that my family and I, collectively and singly, want to eat on a fairly regular basis. Many of them have that comfort factor – in fact, I think that is probably an underlying theme. Some of them are part of a weekly, fortnightly, monthly repertoire. I can guess with pretty good accuracy what any member of my family will want to eat on any given day (taking into account weather, mood, state of wellness, level of hunger) and I suspect I am not alone in that. I hope that, even if my favourites don't coincide completely with yours, there are dishes that are close enough for you to be able to adapt them. I would love everyone who uses this book to develop the confidence to do this – and to be able to convert favourite conventionally cooked recipes too.

PRESSURE-COOKER BASICS

Essentially, a pressure cooker is a saucepan with a weighted and sealed lid, which allows it to build up steam. As the steam builds, the temperature rises and the food cooks much more quickly than if cooked conventionally - on average around 75 per cent faster. And there is no pay-off here. The flavour tends to be better too; I have never known anything for creating depth and pushing flavour through in the way a pressure cooker can. Also, texture - whenever you are cooking meat, the pressure cooker will make quick work of connective tissue, giving body to your stocks, soups and sauces.

For a long time, pressure cookers had something of a reputation. I am going to address that briefly. Older models cooked well, but lacked the safety features of modern ones. The weights were not an integral part of the lid so they could fly off; there was little control over the steam vents and, on models with only one steam vent, if that blocked for any reason, steam would continue building with no outlet and accidents occasionally occurred. But over recent decades, pressure cookers have been completely re-engineered. I don't just mean the electric multicookers which make life very easy by automating part of the process, but the stovetops too are far simpler to use and much safer.

However, like any piece of kitchen equipment, you do have to know how to use a pressure cooker properly and you do need to treat it with respect. Here are a few points that will make the process much easier and more efficient.

1. If you are going to start cooking using oil or fat, heat up your pressure cooker first. This is especially important if your model is stainless steel and you are about to sauté or sear an ingredient or add something starchy, as it will help create a non-stick surface.

2. Before you close the lid to bring up to pressure, make sure the base of the cooker is completely deglazed - ie nothing is sticking to it. If you don't, your cooker may have difficulty coming up to pressure and, in the case of electric pressure cookers, may trigger a burn sensor which will shut it down.

3. Bring your pressure cooker up to pressure as fast as you can, meaning over a high heat. This seems counterintuitive I know, but trust me. The faster the pressure cooker comes up to pressure, the less risk of burning.

NEVER LEAVE A STOVETOP PRESSURE COOKER UNATTENDED WHILE IT IS COMING UP TO PRESSURE.

4. Adjust the heat as soon as your pressure cooker is at pressure (usually high but occasionally low for delicate ingredients such as fish or eggs). You need very little heat to maintain the pressure. If you are using a stovetop, it will take a little trial and error to get this right. I find that most of the time I bring mine up to pressure on my largest ring and it maintains pressure over the lowest heat on my smallest ring, but everyone's model and heat source is different. Of course, if yours is an electric pressure cooker, you don't need to worry about this.

'Zero minutes' is a term you may come across. It means that as soon as the cooker comes up to pressure you immediately remove it from the heat or, in the case of an electric pressure cooker, set the timer to 0.

5. When the pressure cooking time is over, make sure you understand how you need to release the pressure, as it is part of the recipe and affects the cook time. There are three options:

Fast release stops the pressure cooking process immediately. Follow the manufacturer's instructions on how to do this safely. With a stovetop pressure cooker, you can put it in a bowl of cold water or run it under a cold tap which will depressurize the cooker very quickly with a satisfying flump.

Natural release simply involves waiting for the process to drop on its own. A stovetop pressure cooker needs to be removed from the heat, whereas an electric pressure cooker will drop pressure automatically once the timed pressure cooking stops. This is part of the cooking process - it will be coming down from 118-120°C (244-248°F) so will be a while before it hits boiling point and below.

Combined release. Sometimes a recipe will specify leaving it to drop pressure naturally for a specified number of minutes before fast releasing any remaining pressure. Electric pressure cookers have a timer for this.

6. After using your pressure cooker, always clean it properly. Make sure the gasket (rubber seal) is clean and that the vents are not blocked - this is especially important if you have cooked anything starchy.

SOME USEFUL EQUIPMENT

These are the items that I find indispensable:

Timers! If you are using a stovetop pressure cooker you need a timer because some of the timings are very precise - there is often very little between something being just right and being overcooked.

Weighing scales. An obvious one, perhaps, but I measure everything - including liquids - by weight rather than volume. Scales are especially useful when calculating ratios of dried goods to liquid, as I do these by weight too.

Pressure cooker accessories. Most pressure cookers will come with at least one steamer basket, plus a trivet to elevate cake tins, dishes and bowls above the water level. You can also use an upturned steamer basket, or for dishes that can comfortably sit below the water line, a folded piece of cloth or an upturned saucer work as well.

Foil, baking paper and alternatives. Certain things need coating or wrapping in foil or baking paper and I don't use them interchangeably as it impacts a bit on the cook times. A foil sling is very useful if you are taking tight-fitting tins and dishes out of the pressure cooker. To make a reusable sling, simply take a long piece of foil, fold it lengthways several times to form a strong band, then use it to lift things in and out of the cooker, folding down the edges to fit inside as it cooks.

Teflon-coated fabric. I use this when I want to give my pressure cooker a non-stick base. It is heavy enough to stay put if placed on top of a little oil. Perfect for sautéing starchy things like potatoes, or for making potstickers (dumplings), and it can be used many times.

A NOTE ON RECIPE TIMINGS

The recipes in this book are designed to work with a pressure of 12–15PSI/90–103kPa. If your pressure cooker is set lower than this, you may need to increase the timings on some recipes. But I would recommend you try my timings first on the basis it is better to undercook rather than overcook.

Throughout the recipes, in writing the instructions for releasing the pressure I have assumed that a stovetop pressure cooker is used. If you have an electric or a multicooker, do read the manufacturer's instructions.

Happy pressure cooking!

SOUPS

One day I am going to write a whole book devoted to pressure cooker soups. There are people who dislike soup, but I don't understand this at all. Soups are the ultimate in comfort, but they can be anything you like – brothy or thick, smooth or chunky, creamy or spicy or both at the same time. They can be a substantial meal in their own right or a delicate liquid which gives you an excuse to eat lots of buttered toast. I love them all.

You may look at some of the timings for these soups and question their accuracy. I promise you, they are right. It is amazing how quickly a pressure cooker soup can come together. I try to get the balance between ones with fast (almost non-existent) prep and longer cook time, and ones that require a bit more prep and have cook times so short they defy credulity. Not quite as fast as heating up a can or carton, but not far off, and being made from scratch using healthy ingredients, much better for you.

A lot of these recipes have additional garnishes, which I think finish off soups really well but which are of course entirely optional. I often find, with smooth soups in particular, that I want a bit of a variety in texture at some point, which is why I might add a sprinkle of something half-way through if not always at the outset. Garnishes are also a good way of catering to different tastes. Not everyone, for example, will want the bitterness of orange zest added to their carrot soup, so adding it to individual bowls works really well.

TOMATO AND LENTIL SOUP

Serves 4

2 x 400g (14oz) cans tomatoes or the fresh equivalent, puréed

100g (3½oz) red lentils, rinsed

1 onion, halved

10g (¼oz) piece of ginger, roughly chopped

4 garlic cloves

1 tbsp your favourite curry powder or use the basic spice mix (see page 241)

1 tbsp coconut oil

1 litre (35fl oz) vegetable or chicken stock or water

1 small bunch of coriander (cilantro)

Sea salt

A couple of green chillies, finely sliced, to serve

FOR THE TADKA (OPTIONAL)

1 tbsp coconut or olive oil

15 curry leaves

1 tsp mustard seeds or cumin seeds

By far the most popular recipe in my last book was the Buttery Tomato Soup. Here I wanted to create something similar in terms of very fast prep time with the same comfort factor. We are a household that loves spice, so this recipe – inspired by one from Madhur Jaffrey in her excellent *Curry Easy* – does it for us. And it happens to be even faster in terms of prep and cooking!

You don't have to be bound by any of these flavours – it is an excellent receptacle for any spice or curry paste you might want to use up.

Put everything except the coriander and chillies in your pressure cooker. Cut the coriander leaves from the stems and add the stems to the cooker along with plenty of salt, reserving the leaves. Bring to high pressure, then adjust the heat until it is just high enough to maintain the pressure. Cook for 5 minutes, then remove from the heat and leave to drop pressure naturally.

Blitz the soup using a jug or stick blender and make sure it is piping hot. Pour into bowls.

If making the tadka, heat the coconut or olive oil in a small frying pan (skillet) and add the curry leaves and seeds. As soon as they start to crackle and pop, remove from the heat and pour in a swirl over the bowls. Serve with the coriander leaves and some sliced green chillies for extra heat.

PEA AND ASPARAGUS SOUP

Serves 4

15g (½oz) butter

1 leek, trimmed and shredded (include the green bits)

200g (7oz) asparagus trimmings

1 floury potato, peeled and diced (optional)

2 garlic cloves, sliced

250g (9oz) peas (frozen are fine)

Leaves from a large sprig of tarragon

1 strip of pared lime zest, plus a squeeze of lime juice

Sea salt and freshly ground black pepper

TO GARNISH (OPTIONAL)

100g (3½oz) soft goat's cheese or curd

100g (3½oz) cooked asparagus tips (see introduction)

This is a very economical soup for springtime as it is simply dressing up leftovers. During asparagus season, I buy a lot of locally grown asparagus, fresh, and always keep a container in the fridge or freezer for the woodier stems. I sometimes make stock with these, but more often I will use them to make this soup – the asparagus flavour shines through. You can add other bits and pieces to this – for example, any salad leaves that need using up.

I garnish with goat's curd or soft goat's cheese, and sometimes a few asparagus tips. You can simply steam these in the base of your pressure cooker with a splash of water for zero minutes, or you can wrap them in foil, add the trivet to your pressure cooker, and cook at the same time as the soup.

Heat your pressure cooker and add the butter. When melted, add the leek, asparagus trimmings and potato (if using). Stir until everything is glossy with butter, then stir in the garlic, peas, tarragon and lime zest. Season with plenty of salt and pepper if you like. Pour over 600ml (21fl oz) of water (you can use stock if you prefer, but I like the clean flavour from water in this one).

Close the lid and bring up to high pressure. Adjust the heat to just high enough to maintain the pressure. Cook for 2 minutes, then remove from the heat and carefully release the pressure, either in short bursts or a gradual slide.

Fish out the lime zest then blitz the soup until smooth, using a jug or stick blender. If your blender is powerful, it should make short work of the softened asparagus stems, but you can push everything through a sieve if you want to make completely sure (I don't bother – my old Braun stick blender does the job).

Taste for seasoning and add a judicious squeeze of lime juice to bring all the flavours together. Garnish with goat's cheese or curd and asparagus tips, if using.

LENTIL, COURGETTE AND SPINACH SOUP

Serves 4

4 dried apricots (optional)

2 tbsp olive oil

3 garlic cloves, grated (minced)

1 courgette (zucchini), coarsely grated (shredded)

200g (7oz) red lentils

½ tsp ground cinnamon

1 tsp dried mint

8 cubes frozen chopped spinach

100g (3½oz) cherry tomatoes, puréed

1 litre (35fl oz) vegetable or chicken stock

Sea salt and freshly ground black pepper

FOR THE BUTTER

25g (1oz) butter

2 garlic cloves, finely chopped

Zest and juice of 1 lemon

1 tsp dried mint

1 tsp chilli flakes (optional)

This is a very warming soup with a bit of a sweet and sour tang to it, thanks to the inclusion of lemon and also dried apricots. These are entirely optional, but I really like the flavour they add.

If using the apricots, put these in your pressure cooker and cover with water. Close the lid and bring up to high pressure. Immediately remove from the heat and leave to drop pressure naturally. (Softening the apricots in this way makes them much easier to chop.) Remove from the cooker and chop to a purée.

Put all the remaining soup ingredients, including the apricots (if using), into the pressure cooker and season with salt and pepper. Bring to high pressure and adjust the heat until it is just high enough to maintain the pressure. Cook for 2 minutes, then remove from the heat and leave to drop pressure naturally. Taste for seasoning and add the lemon juice.

Melt the butter in a small pan and add the garlic, lemon zest, dried mint and chilli flakes (if using). Season with salt. Serve the soup with spoonfuls of the butter drizzled over.

SWEET POTATO SOUP

Serves 4

1 onion, halved

750g (1lb 10oz) sweet potato, squash or pumpkin, roughly chopped (no need to peel)

5g (⅛oz) piece of ginger, roughly chopped

4 garlic cloves

1 tsp chilli powder or flakes

1 tbsp miso paste (any sort)

Leaves from a few coriander (cilantro) sprigs (optional)

800ml (28fl oz) vegetable or chicken stock or water

Sea salt and freshly ground black pepper

TO FINISH

Juice of 1 orange or mandarin

A rasp of orange or mandarin zest

A drizzle of toasted sesame oil

It is no surprise that soups requiring minimal prep beyond simply putting everything in the pressure cooker and blitzing at the end are incredibly popular. This one uses flavours suggested to me by my friend Sarah Pettegree.

Put everything in the pressure cooker and season with salt and pepper. Bring to high pressure, then adjust the heat until it is just high enough to maintain the pressure. Cook for 5 minutes, then remove from the heat and leave to drop pressure naturally.

Blitz using a jug or stick blender, then strain through a sieve if you would like it extra-smooth.

Stir through the orange juice and rasp over some zest. Serve with a drizzle of toasted sesame oil on each bowl.

HARISSA CARROT SOUP

Serves 4

2 tbsp olive oil

1 onion, roughly chopped

4 large carrots, roughly chopped

1 tbsp harissa paste

1 tsp dried mint

50g (1¾oz) basmati rice, unrinsed

800ml (28fl oz) water or stock

Juice of 1 blood or sweet orange

1 small bunch of flat-leaf parsley, roughly chopped (reserve a few leaves for garnish)

2 tbsp hazelnuts, lightly crushed and toasted, to serve

Sea salt and freshly ground black pepper

FOR THE WHIPPED FETA (OPTIONAL)

200g (7oz) feta

100g (3½fl oz) Greek yogurt

1 tbsp olive or nut oil

1 tsp finely rasped orange zest

As this soup is blended, you don't have to peel the carrots - just make sure they are clean and blemish-free.

The whipped feta is optional - if you are time-pressed, just crumble some in, then drizzle with olive oil and rasp over some orange zest. Or leave it out completely.

Heat your pressure cooker and add the oil. When hot, add all the ingredients up to and including the rice and stir for a couple of minutes. Pour in the water or stock and season with salt and pepper. Stir to make sure the base of the pan is clean.

Close the lid and bring to high pressure, then adjust the heat until it is just high enough to maintain pressure. Cook for 3 minutes, then remove from the heat and leave to drop pressure naturally. Add the blood orange juice and parsley to the cooker and blend using a jug or stick blender. Reheat to make sure it is piping hot.

To make the whipped feta, put the feta and yogurt in a food processor and season with salt and pepper. Blitz until smooth, then, with the motor still running, drizzle in the olive oil. Add the orange zest.

Serve the soup with the whipped feta, if using, a garnish of parsley and a sprinkling of hazelnuts.

CHICKEN
NOODLE SOUP

Serves 4

FOR THE BROTH

4 chicken drumsticks or 2 chicken legs

1 unpeeled small onion, halved

Sprigs of any fresh herbs – bay, tarragon, thyme, oregano, parsley

1 head of garlic, broken into cloves

1 litre (28fl oz) chicken or vegetable stock or water

FOR THE SOUP

500g (1lb 2oz) root vegetables, diced (I prefer carrot and celeriac/celery root)

3 celery sticks, cut into 1cm (½in) slices

3 leeks, trimmed and cut into 2cm (¾in) slices

1 tomato, puréed

50g (1¾oz) noodles – I usually break up spaghetti

A large pinch of saffron, soaked in a little warm water (optional)

Sea salt and freshly ground black pepper

TO SERVE

1 garlic clove, crushed

Leaves from a sprig of tarragon, finely chopped

Leaves from a few sprigs of flat-leaf parsley, finely chopped

Zest and juice of 1 lemon

This is a two-stage recipe and could be made faster still if you already have a decent chicken stock. But I want to show how it is possible to make a soup which has the goodness of homemade chicken stock when you don't have any to hand.

This method takes slightly more time than an all-in-one soup using chicken off the bone. But it will be rich in healthy chicken fat and collagen – exactly the kind of broth I feed my family all winter long to fight off the array of colds and bugs that they inevitably catch.

Put the chicken, onion, herbs and garlic in your pressure cooker with the stock or water. Close the lid and bring up to high pressure. Adjust the heat until it is just high enough to maintain the pressure and cook for 15 minutes. Remove from the heat and leave to drop pressure naturally.

Remove the chicken from the broth. When it is cool enough to handle, pull off the meat and discard everything else. Strain the broth, squashing the flesh from the garlic cloves into the liquid, then return it to the pressure cooker.

Add the chicken meat to the pressure cooker along with all the vegetables, herbs and noodles. If you are using the saffron, add this too, along with the soaking water, then season with plenty of salt and pepper. Bring to high pressure again and adjust the heat to maintain the pressure. Cook for 1 minute, then remove from the heat and leave to drop pressure naturally for 5 minutes. Release any remaining pressure.

Mix the garlic, herbs and lemon zest and juice together and pour this into the soup. Stir and leave to stand for 1 minute. Ladle into bowls and serve.

MUSHROOM AND JERUSALEM ARTICHOKE SOUP

Serves 4

25g (1oz) butter

1 onion, diced

1 large carrot, diced

250g (9oz) Jerusalem artichokes, peeled and diced

250g (9oz) mushrooms, roughly chopped or sliced

4 garlic cloves, crushed or grated (minced)

100g (3½oz) red lentils, unrinsed

1 large sprig of thyme

1 litre (35fl oz) chicken or mushroom stock

Sea salt and freshly ground black pepper

Autumn in a bowl, this. It is without doubt my favourite autumn-into-winter soup and is so popular in my house it has even won over my mushroom-averse stepdaughter. I used to add bacon to it, but left it out once and realized it really doesn't need it – the smoky savouriness of the Jerusalem artichokes make it redundant.

Heat your pressure cooker and add the butter. When melted, add the onion, carrot, artichokes and mushrooms and sauté until the mushrooms have collapsed. Stir in the garlic and red lentils, then add the thyme, salt and pepper and stock. Stir to make sure the base of the cooker is completely deglazed, then close the lid and bring up to high pressure. Adjust the heat to just high enough to maintain the pressure. Cook for 5 minutes, then remove from the heat and leave to drop pressure naturally.

Remove the thyme sprig and serve the soup as is, or give it a very judicious whizz to break it up just a little – or blitz using a jug or stick blender if you prefer it smooth.

CREAMY VEGETABLE SOUP

Serves 4

25g (1oz) butter

1 white onion, roughly chopped

1 large leek, white parts only, finely sliced

250g (9oz) cauliflower florets, chopped

100g (3½oz) white cabbage, shredded

150g (5½oz) potato, peeled and diced

1 bay leaf

A rasping of nutmeg

500ml (17fl oz) vegetable or chicken stock

150ml (5fl oz) single (light) cream

A few chives, finely chopped, to garnish

Sea salt and freshly ground black pepper

This soup is one of those really soothing ones. Savoury, creamy, unchallenging but definitely not bland. And also infinitely adaptable. I use it as a base for a cheese soup, stirring in handfuls of Cheddar or Gruyère, or any other type of cheese I have knocking around, at the end before blitzing. I sometimes add a bacon garnish too but I am very happy with the sting of allium you get from a finely chopped chive.

Heat your pressure cooker and add the butter. When melted, add all the vegetables and the bay leaf. Stir until the vegetables are coated in butter, then season with salt and pepper and grate over some nutmeg. Pour in the stock and give a good stir to make sure nothing is sticking. Bring to high pressure and adjust the heat until it is just high enough to maintain the pressure. Cook for 2 minutes, then fast release.

Fish out the bay leaf and stir in the cream. Blitz using a jug or stick blender and make sure it is piping hot before serving. Garnish with a few chives.

CHICKEN, PUMPKIN AND PEANUT SOUP

Serves 4

1 tbsp coconut or olive oil

1 large onion, finely chopped

1 red (bell) pepper, finely chopped

10g (¼oz) piece of ginger, grated (minced)

4 garlic cloves, grated (minced)

300g (10½oz) chicken thighs, diced

200g (7oz) pumpkin flesh, diced

800ml (28fl oz) chicken or vegetable stock or water

150g (5½oz) peanut butter (crunchy or smooth)

200g (7oz) tomatoes, puréed

1 large sprig of thyme

1 Scotch bonnet, left whole but pierced OR 1 tbsp hot sauce

Sea salt and freshly ground black pepper

TO FINISH

Chopped coriander (cilantro)

Lime wedges

Hot sauce (optional)

I am not exaggerating when I say that I live in a household that is devoted to all things nut butter. My family will eat just about anything that includes it and so they love this soup. The inspiration is, of course, all those African soups and stews which combine peanuts and heat so effectively. Most of these will use freshly roasted and ground nuts, but I honestly think that using a nut butter is just as good.

If you have any Onion, Garlic and Ginger Paste (page 240) in your freezer, you can use 4 cubes of that instead of the fresh equivalent here. This really speeds up your prep time and there is no need to defrost the cubes first, just add with the stock.

Heat your pressure cooker and add the oil. When hot, stir in the onion, red pepper, ginger, garlic, chicken thighs and pumpkin. Stir until the chicken has taken on some colour. Pour some of the stock over the peanut butter, whisking until it has a pourable consistency, then add to the pressure cooker along with all the remaining ingredients, seasoning with salt and pepper. Stir to make sure the base is completely deglazed.

Bring to high pressure, then adjust the heat until it is just high enough to maintain the pressure. Cook for 5 minutes, then fast release. Give the soup a good stir – you should find there are droplets of ochre-coloured oil on top – and leave to stand for a minute or two to settle.

Fish out the Scotch bonnet before ladling into bowls. Serve with a sprinkling of coriander, lime wedges for squeezing and hot sauce if you like. Some brave souls might want to finely chop the discarded Scotch bonnet and add that too.

MY BEST BEEF AND VEGETABLE SOUP

Serves 4

400g (14oz) beef shin

2 tbsp olive oil

30g (1oz) can of anchovies

1 large onion, finely chopped

1 long leek, trimmed and diced

300g (10½oz) carrots, diced

3 celery sticks, diced

200g (7oz) mushrooms, chopped (optional)

1 tsp herbes de Provence

A pinch of chilli flakes (optional)

4 garlic cloves, finely chopped

150ml (5fl oz) red wine

50g (1¾oz) tomato purée

800ml (28fl oz) beef or mushroom stock

Sea salt and freshly ground black pepper

1 small bunch of flat-leaf parsley or mixed herbs, finely chopped, to serve (optional)

The key to this soup is the type of beef you use – a piece of beef shin has a lot of connective tissue, which dissolves into the broth, creating the perfect texture without the need for any other thickeners.

You can add any other root vegetables to this, and some of the more robust greens, such as any of the kales. Other types of green would need to be added after the first pressure cook, but will only need the time it takes to come up to pressure to cook.

First prepare the beef shin. Trim off any really hard, thick pieces of fat but leave the rest. Cut into 1cm (½in) dice.

Heat your pressure cooker and add the oil. When hot, add the beef and brown very quickly. Push to one side and add the anchovies, breaking them up with your wooden spoon. Stir in the vegetables, including the mushrooms if using, and sauté for a couple of minutes. Sprinkle in the herbs and the chilli flakes if using, followed by the garlic.

Pour in the red wine and bring to the boil. Make sure the base of the cooker is completely deglazed then stir in the tomato purée, pour in the stock and season with salt and pepper.

Close the lid and bring up to high pressure, then adjust the heat until it is just high enough to maintain the pressure. Cook for 20 minutes, then remove from the heat and leave to drop pressure naturally.

Stir in the fresh herbs (if using) before serving.

SPINACH SOUP WITH NUTMEG

Serves 4

25g (1oz) butter

1 onion, roughly chopped

1 medium potato, peeled and diced

750g (1lb 10oz) frozen spinach

600ml (21fl oz) vegetable or chicken stock

Zest and juice of ½ lemon

Nutmeg, to taste

50ml (1¾oz) single (light) cream

Sea salt and freshly ground black pepper

Lemon wedges, to serve

A classic, but worth cooking from scratch, especially as it is one of those recipes you probably don't have to shop specially for. I think most people have onion, potato and lemon at hand, and the rest is from the store cupboard or freezer.

Heat your pressure cooker and add the butter. When melted, add the onion and potato. Stir just until the onion and potato are coated in butter, then add the spinach, stock and lemon zest and juice. Season with salt and pepper. Bring to high pressure and immediately remove from the heat. Leave to drop pressure naturally.

Grate in plenty of nutmeg, then blitz using a jug or stick blender. Reheat and add the cream. Taste and add more seasoning and nutmeg if necessary. Serve with a squeeze of lemon juice.

SPLIT PEA AND HAM SOUP

Serves 4

1 small (around 750g/1lb 10oz) piece gammon (uncooked ham), smoked or unsmoked

300g (10½oz) split peas

1 carrot, trimmed and halved

1 onion, halved

1 small or ½ large sweet potato

3 garlic cloves (optional, not every dish has to have garlic)

3 bay leaves

Sea salt and freshly ground black pepper

This soup is one I cook often but it doesn't seem to have made it into a book. It is a 2-in-1 recipe, in that you end up with soup plus a piece of ham for both the soup and for another day – or for a ham sandwich to have alongside the soup. It's also extremely low prep into the bargain. The gammon becomes perfectly tender in the time it takes for the split peas and vegetables to cook while simultaneously providing seasoning and flavour.

As usual, I am going to suggest using this as a blueprint. You can add other spices (I like a whole chilli, thyme and allspice – my favourite Caribbean combination), or other root vegetables or squash.

Put all the ingredients in your pressure cooker with 1.5 litres (52fl oz) of water. Don't add any salt at this stage as you don't know how salty your gammon is, but season with plenty of pepper if you wish.

Close the lid and bring up to high pressure. Adjust the heat until it is just high enough to maintain the pressure. Cook for 10 minutes, then remove from the heat and leave to drop pressure naturally. Remove the ham and the bay leaves from the cooker. Taste for seasoning and add salt if necessary. Blitz the remaining contents to a soup – or you could just simply mash the vegetables; they will break up very easily.

Shred or dice some of the ham and add to the soup before serving – keep the rest for slicing or tearing into chunks to be added to other dishes.

TIP

Check the packaging to see whether you need to soak the ham first. If you do, either leave it in cold water overnight, or you can quick-soak in the cooker. To do this, cover with cold water, close the lid and bring up to high pressure, then immediately fast release. Rinse the meat and discard the water.

ONE-POT
WONDERS

I have stretched the meaning of 'one pot' to include some dishes which have separate elements but which can be cooked together in the same pressure cooker – in a kind of 2-, sometimes even 3-tier cooking system. The classic mince and tatties is an excellent example. The mince is cooked in the base of the cooker, the potatoes above it. So two pots become one, two flames become one... You get the picture: half the washing up, half the fuel, and all done in the time it would take for the potato water to come to the boil.

These are the dishes the pressure cooker is famous for: hearty stews and casseroles, designed to be tasty, filling and comforting yet made in a very short time – minutes rather than the hours normally required by conventional methods.

HEARTY TUSCAN
BEAN SOUP

Serves 4

2 tbsp olive oil

1 onion, finely diced

1 celery stick, finely diced

1 large carrot, diced

4 garlic cloves, finely diced

200g (7oz) butternut squash or pumpkin flesh, diced

250g (9oz) cavolo nero or other type of kale, shredded

200g (7oz) puréed tomatoes, fresh or canned polpa

100ml (3½fl oz) red wine

500g (1lb 2oz) cooked cannellini or borlotti beans (see page 231 for cooking instructions)

1 Parmesan rind (optional)

1 large sprig of thyme or rosemary

2 bay leaves

1 leek, sliced

Sea salt and freshly ground black pepper

TO SERVE

200g (7oz) stale bread, toasted and roughly torn

Parmesan or similar hard cheese, grated (shredded)

This dish – based on ribollita – is packed with vegetables and beans and thickened with bread. If you are using dried, soaked beans and cooking them from scratch (and I hope you are), adding some herbs will help the flavour and you can then use the cooking liquor as the base for your stew too. I would add thyme and bay.

This is a bit of a receptacle dish, so you can add all kinds of vegetables to it – different root vegetables will all work, as will other types of greens.

Heat your pressure cooker and add the oil. When hot, add the onion, celery and carrot and sauté over a high heat for 2–3 minutes, just to get them started. Add 3 of the garlic cloves, the squash and cavolo nero and stir for another minute. Pour over the tomatoes, red wine and 1 litre (35fl oz) of water (or cooking liquor from the beans). Add the beans and season generously with salt and pepper. Tuck in the Parmesan rind, if you have it, along with the herbs. Put the leek on top, close the lid and bring up to high pressure. Adjust the heat so it is just high enough to maintain the pressure and cook for 3 minutes, then remove from the heat and leave to drop pressure naturally.

Fish out the herbs and the remains of the Parmesan rind if you've used it (this can be reused if you freeze it) and mash some of the beans to create a bit of texture. Stir in the remaining garlic for an extra kick.

Divide the bread between bowls and ladle over the soup. Serve sprinkled with Parmesan.

CHICKEN CASSEROLE

Serves 4

2 tbsp olive oil

4 large or 8 small chicken thighs, skin on

100g (3½oz) bacon lardons

1 onion, finely chopped

250g (9oz) button or chestnut mushrooms, halved if large

4 garlic cloves, finely chopped

Leaves from a small bunch of tarragon, finely chopped, plus extra to garnish

150ml (5fl oz) white wine or cider

500g (1lb 2oz) waxy potatoes, sliced if large

12 soft prunes, pitted

100ml (3½fl oz) crème fraîche or soured cream

2 tsp Dijon mustard

2 leeks, trimmed and cut into rounds

Sea salt and freshly ground black pepper

Your choice of greens, such as the Quick-Steamed Greens on page 195, to serve (optional)

Mellow, creamy and comforting, with a sharp little hit from the prunes just to keep it interesting. You can serve any greens with this – most can be added at the same time as the leeks.

The main time drain on this recipe is making sure that the chicken pieces are browned properly. There is a temptation to hover and fiddle, so I would recommend that you get the chicken thighs on and prep everything else while they fry.

Heat your pressure cooker and add the oil. When hot, add the chicken thighs, skin side down, and fry over a medium-high heat until a deep golden brown. Turn over and continue to cook until any skin on the underside has also had a chance to crisp.

Remove the chicken from the cooker. Add the bacon, onion and mushrooms and stir until the lardons have browned. Stir in the garlic and tarragon, then pour in the wine or cider. Deglaze the base of the cooker thoroughly. Return the chicken to the pan and season with salt and pepper. Arrange the potatoes on top and tuck in the prunes.

Close the lid and bring up to high pressure. Adjust the heat so it is just high enough to maintain the pressure, then cook for 6 minutes. Remove from the heat and leave to drop pressure naturally.

Push some of the contents of the cooker to one side so you can easily add the crème fraîche and mustard. Make sure they combine well with the cooking liquor then add the leeks. Return the cooker to high pressure and immediately remove from the heat. Leave to stand for 1 minute, then release the remaining pressure.

Serve with your choice of greens.

FISH AND POTATO CASSEROLE WITH LEMON AND DILL

Serves 4

15g (½oz) butter, plus extra to cook the fish

1 onion, finely chopped

3 garlic cloves, finely chopped or grated (minced)

2 strips of pared lemon zest

2 large sprigs of dill

100ml (3½fl oz) white wine

200ml (7fl oz) chicken, vegetable or fish stock

500g (1lb 2oz) new potatoes, sliced

2 tsp Dijon mustard

100ml (3½fl oz) crème fraîche

2 leeks, trimmed and sliced into rounds

4 x white fish fillets

Sea salt and freshly ground black pepper

OPTIONAL EXTRAS

400g (14oz) mussels, clams or cockles, cleaned and debearded

200g (7oz) green beans or sprouting broccoli, trimmed

TO SERVE

A few fronds of dill, finely chopped

Lemon wedges

This is a quite brothy one-pot which is incredibly fast to put together, so will work well for a quick evening meal. That said, you can elevate it into something even better without much more effort by adding mussels, clams or cockles at the end, as shown here.

Heat your pressure cooker and add the butter. When melted, add the onion and sauté for several minutes until it is taking on a little colour, then stir in the garlic. Add the lemon zest and dill sprigs, then pour in the white wine. Bring to the boil and allow to simmer for 1 minute, then pour in the stock. Add the potatoes and season with salt and pepper.

Close the lid and bring up to high pressure. Cook for 1 minute, then remove from the heat and allow to drop pressure naturally. Stir the mustard and crème fraîche into the potatoes, followed by the leeks. Season the fish with salt and pepper and dot with a little more butter. Lay the fillets over the leeks and, if using, add the shellfish and green beans or sprouting broccoli. Bring up to low pressure and cook for 1 minute. Remove from the heat and leave to stand for 1 minute before slowly releasing the rest of the pressure.

Serve with a sprinkling of dill and lemon wedges for squeezing.

CHICKPEAS
AND PASTA

Serves 4

2 tbsp olive oil

100g (3½oz) smoked bacon lardons

1 large onion, finely diced

3 garlic cloves, finely chopped

1 tsp dried oregano

½ tsp rubbed sage

500g (1lb 2oz) cooked chickpeas
(garbanzo beans)

200g (7oz) canned or fresh tomatoes

500ml (17fl oz) vegetable
or chicken stock

6 cubes frozen spinach (optional)

100g (3½oz) short pasta - I like
ditaloni

Sea salt and freshly ground
black pepper

TO SERVE (OPTIONAL)

Lemon juice

Parmesan, grated

Chilli flakes

This is a thick, comforting potage of a dish, just the thing on a cold day. The version here has bacon, but you can omit it to make this vegetarian, which is just as good - when I do so, I add lots of fresh rosemary in place of the sage and use vegetable stock.

Heat your pressure cooker and add the olive oil. When hot, add the bacon and onion. Sauté until the bacon has crisped up a bit and stir in the garlic. Add all the remaining ingredients and season with salt and pepper.

Make sure the base of the cooker is completely deglazed by stirring thoroughly, then close the lid. Bring to high pressure, then adjust the heat until it is just high enough to maintain the pressure. Cook for 3 minutes, then remove from the heat and leave to drop pressure naturally.

Stir to make sure everything is well combined (if you have used frozen spinach it will need dispersing), then check the seasoning and add a squeeze of lemon. Serve with plenty of Parmesan and give everyone the option of adding chilli flakes at the table.

SAUSAGE MEATBALL CASSEROLE

Serves 4

2 tbsp olive oil

8–12 sausages, depending on appetite

1 onion, finely chopped

100ml (3½fl oz) white wine

1½ tbsp Dijon mustard

200ml (7fl oz) chicken or vegetable stock or water

600g (1lb 5oz) new potatoes, large ones cut into chunks

150g (5½oz) kale (any type), shredded

Sea salt and freshly ground black pepper

OPTIONAL EXTRA

300g (10½oz) frozen petits pois or peas

You can play around with this recipe as much as you like in terms of the type of sausages you use. And, strictly speaking, you don't need to skin them either; it's just that doing so makes the browning process much faster.

If you choose to add peas to bulk out the vegetables, you have two options. You can add them with the potatoes and kale – they will cook to a glorious, soft sweetness. Or, if you want them fresher and greener, add them after the cooking and leave on a low heat for a couple more minutes.

Heat your pressure cooker and add the oil. While it heats, cut each sausage casing lengthways to remove, then divide the sausagemeat into 3 balls. Sear the sausage balls briefly on both sides – this should take moments over a high heat. Remove from the cooker.

Lower the heat to medium and add the onion. Stir for a couple of minutes, then pour in the white wine. Stir vigorously to make sure the base of the cooker is completely deglazed.

Whisk the mustard with the stock or water and pour it into the cooker. Add the potatoes, kale and the peas (if you are including them and you want them soft). Season with salt and pepper. Drop the sausage balls back on top.

Close the lid and bring up to high pressure. Adjust the heat so it is just high enough to maintain the pressure and cook for 5 minutes, then remove from the heat and leave to drop pressure naturally. Add the peas at this stage if you wish; they only need a couple of minutes on a low heat. Serve in shallow bowls.

ONE-POT SAUSAGE AND MUSTARD MASH

Serves 4

1 tbsp olive oil

8 large sausages

2 small red onions, cut into wedges

3 garlic cloves, finely chopped

100ml (3½fl oz) red wine

150ml (5fl oz) chicken or beef stock

1 large sprig of thyme

2 tsp blackberry jelly or lingonberry jam (optional)

Sea salt and freshly ground black pepper

OPTIONAL EXTRA

Your choice of greens, such as 1 Savoy cabbage, shredded

FOR THE MASH

400g (14oz) floury potatoes, peeled and cut into chunks

400g (14oz) celeriac (celery root), peeled and cut into chunks (or add more potato)

1 tbsp wholegrain mustard

25g (1oz) butter

Sausages in a red wine and onion gravy with mash – and even greens if you like – in the same pot. You can use any pork or beef sausage for this, but I also really like venison, which is now readily available in most supermarkets and a good option for its green and high-welfare credentials. If I have some blackberries in the freezer I might throw a handful into the gravy, as well as the jelly.

If you want to add greens to this, there should be room if you are using a deep pressure cooker – a shredded Savoy cabbage would be my choice. Wrap in foil, place on top of the potato and celeriac and then toss in a little butter once the cooking is done.

Heat your pressure cooker and add the oil. When hot, add the sausages and brown on all sides. Remove from the cooker. Add the red onions and sear on the cut sides. Add the garlic and then pour in the red wine. Allow it to come up to the boil and reduce by half. Add the stock and thyme, and season with salt and pepper. Stir to make sure the base of the cooker is completely deglazed, then place the sausages on top.

Place a trivet in the cooker and put a steamer basket on top. Put the potato and celeriac (celery root), if using, in the basket and season with salt. If adding greens, wrap in foil and place on top.

Close the lid and bring up to high pressure. Adjust the heat so it is just high enough to maintain the pressure. Cook for 5 minutes, then remove from the heat and leave to drop pressure naturally. Remove the vegetables, steamer basket and trivet from the cooker. Leave the sausages on a low heat to reduce the gravy if necessary and stir in the jelly or jam if using. Mash the potatoes and celeriac before beating in the mustard and butter.

Serve the sausages and gravy over the mash.

LANCASHIRE HOTPOT

Serves 4

3 tbsp olive oil

750g (1lb 10oz) stewing lamb, cut into large chunks

1 tbsp mustard powder

1 onion, finely sliced

500g (1lb 2oz) carrots, cut into large chunks

2 garlic cloves, finely chopped

A few sprigs of rosemary

100ml (3½fl oz) red wine

Up to 300ml (10½fl oz) beef or lamb stock or water

1 tbsp Worcestershire sauce

600g (1lb 5oz) floury potatoes, unpeeled and thinly sliced

Butter

Sea salt and freshly ground black pepper

You need a bit of fat on the lamb for this dish, but I normally trim off anything that is very thick or hard. I usually use a mixture of meat on and off the bone (you get all the flavour, plus texture too, from the marrow), but off the bone is fine. Traditionally, lamb kidneys were added; if you want to include a couple, brown them along with the meat.

This cooking method doesn't give you a crisp finish on your potatoes, but they will have started to brown and have a good buttery flavour. You can finish off with an air-fryer lid if you have a multicooker, or cover the handles of your pressure cooker with a double layer of foil and put it under a hot grill (broiler).

Heat your pressure cooker and add 2 tablespoons of the oil. Toss the lamb in the mustard powder and season with salt and pepper. Sear the lamb until well browned on all sides, then remove.

Add the remaining oil to the cooker and add the onion. Sauté over a medium heat until starting to soften – you should find that cooking the onion for a few minutes will help deglaze the base after cooking the lamb. Add the carrots, garlic and rosemary. Pour in the red wine and stir to make sure the base of the cooker is completely deglazed. Return the lamb to the cooker.

Pour in just enough stock to almost cover the lamb. Add the Worcestershire sauce, season again, then close the lid. Bring the cooker up to high pressure, then adjust the heat so it is just high enough to maintain the pressure. Cook for 15 minutes, then remove from the heat and leave to drop pressure naturally.

Open the lid and layer the potatoes over the top of the lamb. Season with salt and pepper. Cut a round of baking paper to fit snugly in the pressure cooker: scrunch it up then open it again so it will lie flat. Butter generously and place, butter side down, on the potatoes.

Close the lid. Bring up to high pressure again and cook for 1 minute. Remove from the heat and leave to drop pressure naturally again.

Leave to stand for 10 minutes – it will thicken slightly – before serving.

PORK AND CIDER COBBLER

Serves 4

1 tbsp olive oil

1 large onion, thickly sliced

750g (1lb 10oz) diced pork

2 tsp mustard powder

250g (9oz) celeriac (celery root), cut into wedges

250g (9oz) carrots, cut into chunks

3 garlic cloves, finely chopped

2 tsp dried sage

250ml (9fl oz) cider

100g (3½oz) kale leaves, roughly torn

2 tbsp crème fraîche

1 tbsp wholegrain mustard

Sea salt and freshly ground black pepper

FOR THE COBBLER TOPPING

150g (5½oz) self-raising flour

125g (4½oz) fine or medium-fine cornmeal

1 tsp baking powder

75g (2½oz) butter, chilled and diced

1 small eating apple, grated (shredded)

75g (2½oz) hard cheese, such as Cheddar, Manchego, Gruyère, grated (shredded)

1 tsp dried sage

75ml (2¾fl oz) buttermilk

1 egg

There are options with this recipe. You can make it as written as a cobbler. Or you can forget about the topping and serve it as a casserole instead – it will be excellent with a mound of mashed potato. If this is your preferred option, increase the initial cook time to 15 minutes, and cut the eating apple into wedges and add to the casserole instead of the cobbler topping. Oh, and you can cook some potatoes in a steamer basket set over the top if you like – follow the Sausage and Mustard Mash recipe on page 41.

Heat your pressure cooker and add the oil. When hot, add the onion and sauté for 2–3 minutes, just to get it started. Toss the pork in the mustard powder and add to the cooker. Stir until lightly browned on all sides. Add the celeriac, carrots and garlic, then sprinkle in the dried sage and stir. Pour over the cider and stir to make sure the base of the cooker is completely deglazed. Season with salt and pepper.

Close the lid and bring up to high pressure. Adjust the heat so it is just high enough to maintain the pressure and cook for 10 minutes, then remove from the heat and leave to drop pressure naturally. Open the cooker and stir in the kale, crème fraîche and mustard.

While the pork is cooking, make the cobbler topping. Put the flour, cornmeal and baking powder into a bowl with a pinch of salt and rub in the butter. Stir in the apple, cheese and sage. Mix the buttermilk and egg together and add to the dry ingredients. Work together until you have a firm dough. Divide the dough into 12–16 pieces and flatten slightly.

Arrange the discs of dough over the top of the casserole. Leave on a low heat for 5 minutes, then close the lid, bring up to high pressure again and cook for 5 more minutes. Natural release for 5 minutes, then release any remaining pressure. Serve immediately.

NEEPS AND HAGGIS

Serves 4

1 swede (rutabaga), peeled and cut into 1cm (½in) dice

4 carrots, diced

750g (1lb 10oz) floury potatoes, peeled or not

1 haggis, meat or vegetarian (around 450g/1lb), outer packaging removed

50g (1¾oz) butter

Sea salt and freshly ground black pepper

TIP

Any leftovers make really good little haggis cakes, especially if you have potato. Mix all the leftovers together along with any cooked greens you might have. Shape into flat rounds the size of an average fishcake. Dust in seasoned flour, dip first into beaten egg, then into breadcrumbs. Shallow-fry in oil, lard or butter until well browned on both sides and piping hot inside. These are really good with brown sauce.

The traditional time to eat this Scottish delicacy is on Burns Night, but it has become a popular quick meal in our house. My family all love haggis, especially with crushed, buttery carrots and swede. I wanted to show how you can heat a shop-bought haggis in the same pot that the root veg are cooked in and, if your pressure cooker is deep enough, the potatoes too. Haggis is sold ready-cooked but takes ages to reheat conventionally - the recommended oven time is 75 minutes - so you are saving a lot of time and fuel, even without taking into account cooking the carrots and swede in the same pot.

Pour around 2cm (¾in) of water into your pressure cooker and add the trivet. Put the steamer basket on top with the swede and carrots on one half (the swede below the carrot) and the potatoes in the other half. (If you have steamer basket dividers, these are useful here to keep everything separate. You could also fold up a piece of foil into a strip and use that instead.) Wrap the haggis loosely in foil and place on top.

Close the lid, bring up to high pressure and adjust the heat so it is just high enough to maintain the pressure. Cook for 15 minutes, then remove from the heat and allow to drop pressure naturally.

Remove the haggis from the pressure cooker and set aside. Transfer the swede and carrots to a bowl and the potatoes to another. Divide the butter between the two and add plenty of salt and pepper. Mash the potato and lightly crush the carrot and swede.

Transfer the crushed swede and carrot and the mashed potato to a warm serving bowl. Unwrap the haggis and pierce the casing - it will have swollen to a tautness which makes it very satisfying to pierce. It will split and the filling will gently burst out. Put in a separate bowl or spoon over the vegetables and serve immediately.

MINCE
AND TATTIES

Serves 4

1 tbsp olive oil

500g (1lb 2oz) minced (ground) beef
(or lamb if you prefer)

1 large onion, finely diced

2 carrots, diced

2 celery sticks, diced (optional)

1 tbsp mustard powder or plain
(all-purpose) flour

2 tbsp tomato purée

1 tbsp Worcestershire sauce

1 tsp dried thyme

250ml (9fl oz) beef stock

2 tsp Bovril or similar (optional)

Sea salt and freshly ground
black pepper

FOR THE POTATOES

800g (1lb 12oz) floury potatoes,
peeled (optional) and diced

25g (1oz) butter

50ml (1¾fl oz) milk (optional)

The key to this dish is the meat. You really need mince with a high fat content; I would go for at least 10%. This not only vastly improves the texture of the sauce, but also helps tenderize the mince. Very lean mince does not like to tenderize, no matter how long you cook it.

Don't limit yourself to the ingredients listed here. If you want to add a bit of swede or turnip, or the dregs of a bottle of red, you can. I like a bit of Bovril in mine to ramp up the umami, but you could also use soy or fish sauce.

I think most people would want mash with their mince, but I have given the option of cooking with the skins on and just crushing (actually, squashing), as I prefer the texture and I don't like losing the nutritional content by peeling.

Heat your pressure cooker and add the oil. When hot, add the minced beef and sear on one side before stirring. Break it up with your wooden spoon and continue to sear and turn until it is cooked through and some of the fat has rendered out.

Add the vegetables to the cooker and cook for another couple of minutes. Stir in the mustard powder or flour, the tomato purée, Worcestershire sauce and thyme. Pour in the stock and stir thoroughly to make sure the base of the cooker is completely deglazed. Season with salt and pepper. Taste and add a little Bovril for flavour.

Place a trivet in the pressure cooker and put a steamer basket on top so it sits above the mince. Put the potatoes in the steamer basket.

Close the lid and bring up to high pressure. Adjust the heat so it is just high enough to maintain the pressure. Cook for 10 minutes, then remove from the heat and leave to drop pressure naturally.

Remove the potatoes, the steamer basket and the trivet from the cooker. Leave the mince on a low heat if you think the liquid needs to reduce a bit before serving. Mash the potatoes with the butter and milk, or simply crush and mix with butter as I mention above.

Serve the mince as a thick gravy over the tatties.

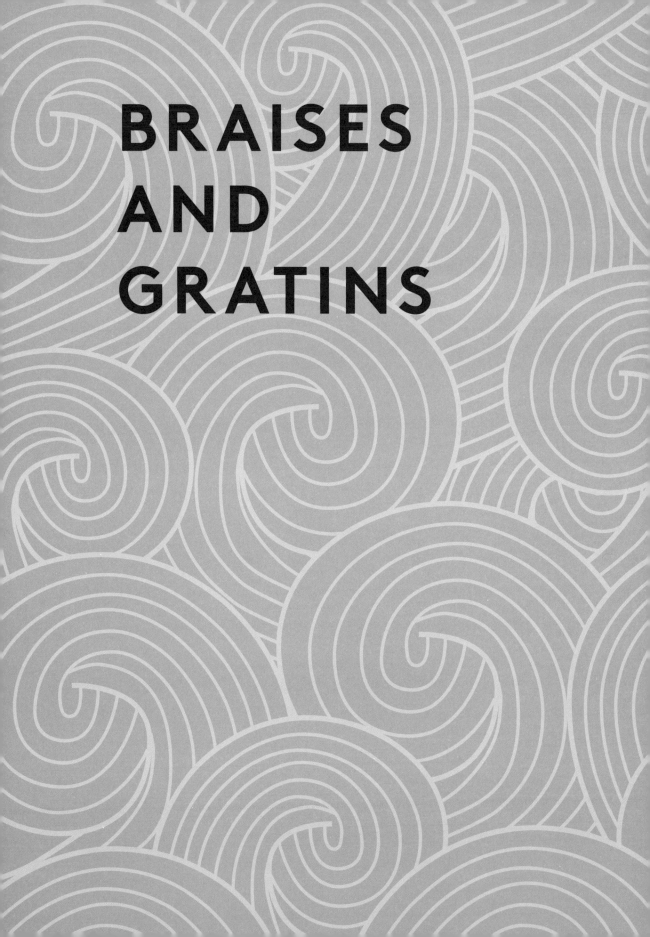

BRAISES AND GRATINS

I shouldn't play favourites, but some of the recipes in this chapter are up there for me. I love the whole concept of braising: it is such a gentle process. Braises are such low effort and take no time at all to cook - a quick sauté in oil, then a brief simmer in a little liquid - so win win. Gratins too I cook on repeat, finishing them under the grill if I want a crisp topping. If you try nothing else from this chapter, please make the onion gratin - and the soup it can transform into.

In many of these recipes, the amount of meat can be reduced substantially in favour of more beans or vegetables - in this way the meat takes on a supporting role, acting to flavour the other ingredients rather than dominating the cast.

CHICKEN WITH CHORIZO

Serves 4

2 tbsp olive oil

150g (5½oz) spicy cooking chorizo, sliced into rounds

1 red onion, cut into wedges

1 red (bell) pepper, cut into thick strips

3 garlic cloves, finely chopped (optional)

6 skinless chicken thigh fillets, halved

1 tsp dried thyme

100ml (3½fl oz) white or red wine

200g (7oz) tomatoes, fresh or canned, puréed

400g (14oz) salad potatoes, thickly sliced

Sea salt and freshly ground black pepper

OPTIONAL EXTRA

400g (14oz) sprouting broccoli or green beans, trimmed

TO SERVE

1–2 tsp sherry vinegar

Zest and juice of ½ lemon

1 small bunch of flat-leaf parsley, finely chopped

When I was writing this book, I talked to as many people as I could about how they cook and eat - even setting up little WhatsApp focus groups. The ingredients that came up more than any others were chicken and chorizo, often together. This makes so much sense to me - chorizo is one of those big flavour ingredients which can carry a dish, meaning there is less need for other seasonings. That is why the garlic is optional in this recipe - there is already quite a whack in the chorizo.

Heat your pressure cooker and add the oil. When hot, add the chorizo and sear on both sides. Remove and add the onion and pepper. Sauté for 1 minute over a high heat then add the garlic and cook for a further minute. Push to one side and add the chicken. Stir to coat it with the ochre-coloured oil, then sprinkle over the thyme.

Pour in the wine and stir to make sure the base of the cooker is completely deglazed. Spread the chicken evenly over the cooker, then add the tomatoes, 100ml (3½fl oz) of water and the potatoes. Season generously. Return the chorizo to the cooker, placing it on top of the potatoes. If you want to cook some greens to serve alongside, wrap in foil and place in the cooker.

Close the lid and bring up to high pressure. Adjust the heat so it is just high enough to maintain the pressure, then cook for 3 minutes. Remove from the heat and leave to drop pressure naturally.

Stir in the sherry vinegar, a teaspoon at a time, tasting as you go, then do the same with the lemon juice. Sprinkle over the lemon zest and parsley and serve immediately.

CIDER-BRAISED SMOKED SAUSAGES

Serves 4

2 tbsp olive oil

1 small cabbage, cut into wedges

400g (14oz) smoked kielbasa, cut into chunks on the diagonal

1 onion, cut into thin wedges

250g (9oz) mushrooms, halved if large

3 garlic cloves, finely chopped

15g (½oz) dried mushrooms, soaked in 100ml (3½fl oz) warm water

250ml (9fl oz) cider

1 tbsp Dijon mustard

100ml (3½fl oz) crème fraîche

Sea salt and freshly ground black pepper

TO SERVE (OPTIONAL)

200g (7oz) cooked barley or spelt (see page 233 for cooking instructions)

Finely chopped flat-leaf parsley or dill

I make this with fat kielbasa from my local Polish grocers. Most supermarkets also have them, or you could use something like chorizo or a saucisse de Morteau. I can happily eat this on its own, but it is good with mashed potatoes or cooked barley or spelt.

Heat your pressure cooker and add the oil. When hot, add the cabbage wedges and sear on both cut sides. Remove from the cooker. Add the kielbasa and sear on all sides, then push to one side and add the onion and mushrooms. Cook for several minutes until the mushrooms have released their liquid and it has evaporated. Stir in the garlic.

Strain the soaked mushrooms, reserving their soaking liquid but make sure you discard any gritty residue. Finely chop the mushrooms and add to the cooker, along with the liquid, cider and mustard. Stir to make sure the base of the cooker is completely deglazed. Season with salt and pepper. Roughly chop the seared cabbage wedges and place on top.

Close the lid and bring up to high pressure. Adjust the heat so it is just high enough to maintain the pressure and cook for 1 minute. Fast release.

Stir in the crème fraîche and leave to simmer for a couple of minutes. Serve alongside some cooked grain, sprinkled with chopped herbs.

AUBERGINE AND BUTTER BEAN BRAISE

Serves 4

3 tbsp olive oil

1 large aubergine (eggplant),
or, preferably, 2 smaller ones,
around 300g (10½oz), cut into
2.5cm (1in) dice

2 medium red onions, cut into wedges

4 garlic cloves, finely chopped

1 tsp dried mint

¼ tsp ground cinnamon

50ml (1¾fl oz) white wine

500g (1lb 2oz) cooked butter (lima)
beans (see page 231 for cooking
instructions)

200g (7oz) tomatoes (canned or
fresh), puréed

200g (7oz) block of halloumi, sliced

300g (10½oz) green beans, trimmed
(optional)

Sea salt and freshly ground
black pepper

TO SERVE

Good olive oil

Finely chopped flat-leaf parsley

A rasping of lemon zest

So simple this, a bit Greek-inspired, what with the mint, cinnamon and butter beans. It needs nothing more than maybe some bread or a green (or Greek) salad but I have also added some optional green beans to cook on top, if you don't want to go to the bother of making a salad.

Heat your pressure cooker and add 2 tablespoons of the oil. When hot, add the aubergine and fry quickly until the cut edges have browned. Push to one side and add the remaining oil and the onions. Cook for a couple of minutes, then add the garlic and cook for another minute.

Stir the aubergines and onions together then sprinkle over the mint and cinnamon. Pour in the wine and stir to deglaze the base of the cooker. Add the butter beans and tomatoes and season with salt and pepper. Stir and give the cooker a little shake so everything falls evenly. Arrange the halloumi on top. If using green beans, wrap loosely in foil and put into the cooker.

Close the lid and bring up to high pressure. Adjust the heat so it is just high enough to maintain the pressure and cook for 2 minutes, then remove from the heat and leave to drop pressure naturally.

Ladle into bowls and drizzle over some olive oil and finish with a sprinkle of parsley and lemon zest.

BRAISED BARLEY WITH CHICKEN

Serves 4 as a risotto, 6 as a soup

1 tbsp olive oil

1 onion, finely chopped

2 large carrots, cut into matchsticks

400g (14oz) chicken meat, preferably thigh, diced

2 garlic cloves, finely chopped

½ tsp ground turmeric

1 tsp ground allspice

1 tsp ground cinnamon

1 tsp dried mint

300g (10½oz) pearled barley

600ml (21fl oz) chicken stock

100g (3½oz) fresh spinach (or 4 frozen cubes)

Sea salt and freshly ground black pepper

TO FINISH

1 small bunch of flat-leaf parsley, finely chopped

100g (3½fl oz) yogurt

A squeeze of lemon or lime juice

The inspiration for this was sup e jow, Persian barley and carrot soup, which I have risottofied, adding chicken as well. You can easily turn it back into a very hearty soup if you want to - just add another 500ml (17fl oz) of stock or water.

Heat your pressure cooker and add the oil. When hot, add the onion and fry briskly without stirring until the onion has started to catch around the edges (not stirring means this will happen more quickly). Add the carrot and chicken. Stir until the chicken has coloured, then stir in the garlic, the spices, mint and barley. Season with plenty of salt and pepper, pour in the stock and stir to make sure the base of the cooker is completely deglazed. If using frozen spinach, drop the blocks into the cooker.

Close the lid and bring up to high pressure. Adjust the heat so it is just high enough to maintain the pressure, then cook for 12 minutes. Remove from the heat and leave to drop pressure naturally.

Open the cooker. If using fresh spinach, push it into the pot until it collapses down, then stir in most of the parsley. Ladle into bowls and serve with dollops of yogurt, a sprinkling of the remaining parsley and a squeeze of citrus juice.

SPICED LAMB AND AUBERGINES

Serves 4

3 tbsp olive oil

1 large aubergine (eggplant),
cut into bite-sized chunks

1 onion, finely chopped

400g (14oz) minced (ground) lamb

4 garlic cloves, crushed or grated
(minced)

2 tbsp harissa (I like a smoked one)

2 tbsp tomato purée

500g (1lb 2oz) cooked chickpeas
(garbanzo beans) or cooked dried
fava beans (see page 231 for cooking
instructions)

Juice of 1 lemon

Sea salt and freshly ground
black pepper

Finely chopped flat-leaf parsley,
to serve

FOR THE SPICES (OPTIONAL)

½ tsp ground cinnamon

½ tsp ground allspice

½ tsp ground turmeric

FOR THE SAUCE (OPTIONAL)

3 tbsp tahini

Zest and juice of 1 lemon

1 garlic clove, crushed

2 tbsp yogurt

½ tsp honey

I love the combination of lamb and aubergines and this is one of my favourite ways to pair them. If I have preserved lemons (the quick method on page 238 works a treat), I might finely chop some into this dish as well.

For something on the side, try the Bulgar Wheat Pilaf on page 208. You could also serve with flatbreads, pitta or rice.

If you are using the spices, mix them together and add plenty of freshly ground black pepper. Set aside.

Heat your pressure cooker and add 2 tbsp of the oil. When hot, add the aubergine and leave for a couple of minutes or so until browned underneath. Stir until lightly browned on all sides then remove and set aside.

Heat the remaining olive oil in the cooker and add the onion and minced lamb. Sauté over a high heat until the meat is well browned, then stir in the garlic, harissa, tomato purée, chickpeas or fava beans and a teaspoon of the spices. Return the aubergine, salt well, and pour in 200ml (7fl oz) of water. Stir thoroughly to make sure the base of the cooker is completely deglazed.

Close the lid and bring up to high pressure. Adjust the heat so it is just high enough to maintain the pressure, then cook for 2 minutes. Remove from the heat and leave to drop pressure naturally. Add lemon juice to taste.

If you are including the sauce, mix the ingredients together with just enough water to give it the consistency of unwhipped double (heavy) cream.

Sprinkle the lamb with the parsley and the remaining spices. Serve with the tahini sauce, if using.

BRAISED FISH WITH CHICKPEAS

Serves 4

2 tbsp olive oil, plus extra to drizzle

1 red onion, diced

4 garlic cloves, finely sliced

A few sprigs of rosemary

1 tsp chilli flakes

2 tsp North African-style spice mix (see page 241), or ras-el-hanout

500g (1lb 2oz) cooked chickpeas (garbanzo beans) – see page 231 for cooking instructions

100ml (3½fl oz) white wine

400g (14oz) fresh or canned tomatoes, puréed

4 white fish steaks or thick pieces of loin, eg hake, halibut, cod or coley (or one whole fish, cleaned and gutted)

Zest and juice of 1 lemon

200g (7oz) baby leaf spinach (optional)

Sea salt and freshly ground black pepper

Finely chopped flat-leaf parsley, to serve (optional)

This is a one-pot, but cooked in two parts. The chickpeas are cooked in a sauce first to allow the flavours to develop, then the fish is added and cooked quickly but gently on top. It takes moments to put together and just a few minutes to cook.

I usually use thick pieces of loin or steaks here, but I have also tested this with a whole white fish, trimmed to fit, and it braised perfectly in the time. It is more fiddly to serve, but more of a show-stopper.

Heat your pressure cooker and add the oil. When hot, add the red onion, sauté for a few minutes, just to get it started, then stir in the garlic, rosemary, chilli flakes and spice mix. Add the chickpeas, then pour in the white wine and tomatoes. Season with salt and pepper and stir to make sure the base of the cooker is completely deglazed.

Close the lid and bring up to high pressure. Adjust the heat so it is just high enough to maintain the pressure, then cook for 5 minutes. Remove from the heat and fast release.

Season the fish and, if cooking a whole one, cut a few slashes into the flesh. Arrange on top of the chickpeas and close the lid. Bring up to low pressure, cook for 2 minutes, then remove from the heat and leave to drop pressure for another 3 minutes. Release the remaining pressure.

Remove the fish from the pan. Squeeze over some lemon juice and stir the zest into the chickpeas. If using spinach, add now and stir until wilted into the sauce. Divide the chickpeas between bowls and top each one with a fish steak (or present a whole fish at the table). Drizzle with a little more olive oil and garnish with chopped parsley, if you like.

POTATO AND CAMEMBERT GRATIN

Serves 4

1 tbsp olive oil

15g (½oz) butter

500g (1lb 2oz) Brussels sprouts, trimmed and halved

1 onion, finely chopped

300g (10½oz) mushrooms (any sort), roughly chopped

500g (1lb 2oz) potatoes, halved lengthways and thinly sliced

3 garlic cloves, finely chopped

½ tsp herbes de Provence

150ml (5fl oz) white wine

100ml (3½fl oz) crème fraîche

1 tsp Dijon mustard

100g (3½oz) Gruyère, grated (shredded)

1 x 250g (9oz) Camembert or similar rinded cheese, fridge cold

Sea salt and freshly ground black pepper

This is exactly what you need on a cold day. I have made it vegetarian, but there is nothing to stop you frying up a bit of bacon with the onion, or adding chunks of ham along with the potatoes. Or, you could serve thick slices of either on the side...

Heat your pressure cooker and add the olive oil and butter. When hot, add the Brussels sprouts and fry until lightly browned on the cut side. Remove. Add the onion and mushrooms. Fry over a high heat until both are starting to brown around the edges and the mushrooms start to collapse. If they begin to release liquid (a sign of a slightly crowded pan), keep cooking until it has evaporated.

Stir in the potatoes and garlic and sauté for another couple of minutes. Sprinkle in the herbs, then add the wine. Stir to make sure the base of the cooker is completely deglazed, then return the sprouts to the cooker. Season with salt and pepper. Mix the crème fraîche with the mustard and stir this into the cooker along with the Gruyère.

Slice the Camembert into four rounds – the last couple might get a little messy, but it doesn't matter – then arrange over the vegetables.

Close the lid and bring up to high pressure. Adjust the heat so it is just high enough to maintain the pressure and cook for 2 minutes, then remove from the heat and leave for 1 minute before releasing the remaining pressure. Remove the lid and leave over a low heat for a few minutes to allow the sauce to thicken a little.

You can serve just as it is – my preference – or you can brown the top by covering the handles of the cooker and putting under a preheated grill (broiler), or by using an air-fryer lid or blowtorch.

MY BEST ONION GRATIN (AND SOUP)

**Serves 4 (as a gratin)
or 2 with enough for soup the next day**

6-8 medium onions, depending on size and space

2 tbsp olive oil

1 tsp herbes de Provence or dried thyme

Leaves from a large sprig of tarragon, finely chopped (optional)

1 tbsp sherry vinegar

100ml (3½fl oz) white wine, dry sherry or vermouth

100ml (3½fl oz) crème fraîche

100g (3½oz) Gruyère, coarsely grated (shredded)

Sea salt and freshly ground black pepper

FOR THE TOPPING

15g (½oz) butter

75g (2½oz) coarse breadcrumbs

2 tbsp finely chopped flat-leaf parsley

Generous pinch of chilli flakes (optional)

This is a recipe that gives you options, some of which I give at the end of the method, but usually what I do is make this using 8 onions, halved widthways, which just about fit into a 24cm (9½in) diameter pressure cooker, and serve 3-4 halves each to me and my husband for lunch. I then blitz the rest - and I don't say this lightly - into what might be the best-ever onion soup for the following day. Two lunches made in less than 20 minutes, start to finish.

First prepare the onions. Peel them carefully, leaving as much of the root intact as possible as you don't want them to fall apart when they cook. Cut in half widthways (not from root to stem), so all the rings are visible.

Heat your pressure cooker and add the oil. You need the oil to be hot for this - if you have an electric pressure cooker which has a very sensitive heat detector/burn sensor, you might want to do this stage in a frying pan (skillet). When the oil is hot, place the onions, cut side down, on the base of the cooker and sear for several minutes. I usually set the timer and walk away for 4-5 minutes, so I don't fiddle with them too much. When they have developed a decent colour - the dark side of caramel - flip over (or transfer, cut side up, to the cooker). Sprinkle with the herbs and season with salt and pepper. Carefully drizzle the sherry vinegar over the onions - any that hits the base of the cooker will hiss and splutter. Pour the alcohol around the onions and immediately put the lid on. You should find a lot of steam is created and that the pressure will consequently rise very quickly. Adjust the heat so it is just high enough to maintain the pressure and cook for 3 minutes. Remove from the heat and leave to drop pressure naturally.

While the onions are cooking, make the topping. Heat the butter in a frying pan until it foams, then add the breadcrumbs. Stir until all the

CONTINUED . . .

MY BEST ONION GRATIN
(AND SOUP) CONTINUED . . .

butter has been absorbed and the breadcrumbs have started to crisp up. Stir through the parsley and the chilli flakes, if using.

Add the crème fraîche to the cooker and gently swirl so it combines with the pan juices.

Now you have two options. You can sprinkle with cheese and just cover and leave over a low heat to melt – this is what I usually do. Or you can transfer to a gratin dish, sprinkle with the cheese and put under a hot grill (broiler) or use an air-fryer lid if you have one. Either way, sprinkle with the breadcrumb mixture and serve.

WHAT TO DO WITH THESE ONIONS

- Serve them as a light meal with bread, with perhaps a tomato salad on the side.

- Serve them as a side dish – especially good with roast chicken or a pork chop.

- Break them up before you add the cheese and stir them and the cheese through some pasta.

- Blitz until smooth and add chicken or vegetable stock for an excellent soup. A half portion of these onions will need 600ml (21fl oz) of stock. You can add the cheese to the soup or sprinkle it on baguette slices to serve with the soup.

GENTLY SPICED CHICKEN WITH VEGETABLES

Serves 4

2 tbsp olive oil

1 onion, roughly chopped

1-2 chicken thigh fillets per person, skinned and halved

2 garlic cloves, finely chopped

2 tsp ras-el-hanout (or the North African-style spice mix on page 241)

2 tomatoes, puréed (fresh are better than canned here)

A pinch of saffron, soaked in a little warm water

150ml (5fl oz) chicken or vegetable stock or water

400g (14oz) broad (fava) beans or peas

250g (9oz) broccoli or romesco cauliflower, cut into small chunks

2 medium courgettes (zucchini), sliced

Lemon juice

1 small bunch of mint or dill leaves, chopped

Sea salt and freshly ground black pepper

Couscous or your choice of grain, to serve

This is one of those dishes that can be thrown together in 5 minutes, or it can take much longer if you decide to double-pod the broad beans. I don't bother skinning the frozen ones as they are very small and tender and the skins don't have the tannic bitterness of larger ones. But it is up to you.

Heat your pressure cooker and add the oil. When hot, add the onion and chicken and turn over in the oil until the chicken is lightly coloured. Stir in the garlic and spices, followed by the tomatoes and the saffron and its soaking water. Mix to combine and season with salt and pepper. Pour in the stock or water and give a quick stir to make sure the base is deglazed. Close the lid and bring up to high pressure. Immediately remove from the heat and leave to drop pressure naturally.

Add the remaining vegetables and season with salt and pepper. Bring up to high pressure again and remove from the heat. Leave to stand for 1 minute before fast releasing the remaining pressure.

Add lemon juice to taste and finish with the herbs. Serve with couscous.

SAUSAGE AND SQUASH GRATIN

Serves 4

2 tbsp olive oil

500g (1lb 2oz) prepared squash (seeds removed and cut into slim wedges)

1 onion, thickly sliced

4 sausages, skinned

2 garlic cloves, finely chopped

200g (7oz) kale, shredded

1 tsp dried thyme

100ml (3½fl oz) white wine

250g (9oz) cooked white beans, such as cannellini (optional) – see page 231 for cooking instructions

2 tsp maple syrup

1 tbsp Dijon or wholegrain mustard

150ml (5fl oz) crème fraîche

Sea salt and freshly ground black pepper

FOR THE TOPPING

1 tbsp olive oil or butter

25g (1oz) breadcrumbs

25g (1oz) pecans, finely chopped

1 garlic clove, finely chopped

Finely chopped flat-leaf parsley

This dish doesn't have much meat in it, relatively speaking, and you can reduce/increase the amount as you like. I find it substantial as it is, but you have the option of adding beans for a more carb-heavy meal.

I use a small onion squash (red kuri) for this, but any squash with edible skin and reasonably firm flesh will work – you could use butternut squash if you like.

Heat your pressure cooker and add half the oil. When hot, sear the squash wedges on each cut side, then remove from the cooker and cut in half widthways. Add the remaining oil, then the onion and sausages. Roughly break up the sausages with a spoon – don't make them too small – and brown, stirring regularly.

Stir in the garlic and kale and cook until the kale wilts a little. Sprinkle in the thyme and wine. Stir to deglaze the base of the cooker thoroughly, then add the beans, if using. Mix the maple syrup, mustard and crème fraîche together and thin with 50ml (1¾fl oz) of water. Pour into the cooker and give everything a quick stir. Return the squash wedges to the cooker and season with salt and pepper.

Close the lid and bring up to high pressure. Adjust the heat so it is just high enough to maintain the pressure and cook for 3 minutes, then leave to drop pressure naturally.

Meanwhile, prepare the topping. Heat the oil or butter in a frying pan (skillet) and add the breadcrumbs and pecans. Toast until they smell rich and nutty, then stir in the garlic and parsley. Remove from the heat and season with salt and pepper.

Sprinkle the topping over the dish and leave to stand for a few minutes before serving.

QUINOA AND CORN PILAF

Serves 4

1 tbsp olive oil

Kernels from 1 large or 2 medium corn on the cob

1 courgette (zucchini), diced

2 garlic cloves, crushed

1 tsp dried mint

200g (7oz) quinoa, well rinsed and drained

200g (7oz) block of halloumi or feta, diced

100g (3½oz) small seedless grapes (green or red)

Sea salt and freshly ground black pepper

FOR THE DRESSING

4 semi-dried tomatoes (smoked if possible)

3 tbsp olive oil (or use the oil from the tomato jar)

1 garlic clove

1 tbsp sherry vinegar

A few basil leaves

1 tsp smoked or hot paprika (optional)

TO SERVE

3 spring onions (scallions), shredded

A few basil leaves

This is very light and comforting at the same time. I especially love how the halloumi softens to a creamy squidginess. You can of course grill or fry it separately instead – we are used to it having a crust, after all – but here I think it works better this way. You can also use feta (it will cook to a mellow creaminess and break up as soon as you go near it), which will be very different to the halloumi, but no less good.

If you can get a jar of smoked semi-dried tomatoes (I love the Isle of Wight ones), they make a superb dressing, but using a smoked paprika will give a similar flavour, so if you can't get any, the dish will still taste as it should. Serve on its own or with a salad of floppy green lettuce.

Heat your pressure cooker and add the oil. When hot, add the corn kernels (be careful, they may splutter) and stir-fry for a minute or two until they start to take on some colour. Add the courgette and fry for a further couple of minutes, then stir in the garlic and mint.

Add the quinoa to the cooker and stir for another minute or two – lightly toasting it like this improves the flavour no end. Season with salt and pepper, then pour in 250ml (9fl oz) of water and stir to make sure the base of the cooker is completely deglazed. Drop the halloumi or feta and grapes over the top.

Close the lid and bring up to high pressure. Adjust the heat so it is just high enough to maintain the pressure, then cook for 1 minute only. Remove from the heat and leave to drop pressure naturally.

While the quinoa is cooking, make the dressing. Whizz everything together in a small food processor with some salt and pepper.

Serve the pilaf in bowls with the dressing drizzled over and a sprinkling of spring onions and basil leaves.

QUICK EGGS
AND BEANS

Serves 2-4

2 tbsp olive oil

100g (3½oz) spicy chorizo, diced
(or any type of bacon/sausage)

1 red or white onion, cut into wedges

1 red or green (bell) pepper, diced

400g (14oz) canned tomatoes

250g (9oz) cooked beans – white,
black, butter (lima), pinto (see page
231 for cooking instructions)

2 tsp sherry vinegar

4 eggs

100g (3½oz) hard cheese, such
as Cheddar or Manchego, grated
(shredded)

Sea salt and freshly ground
black pepper

GREEN SAUCE (OPTIONAL)

3 tbsp olive oil

1 small bunch of coriander (cilantro)

Zest and juice of 1 lemon or lime

1 garlic clove

This is the kind of dish I cook when I don't know what to make as it is made of ingredients I pretty much always have in the house. And if I don't, then I can substitute - a courgette in place of the pepper, or even a big pile of kale, is just one example.

This is enough to feed 2 generously, 4 much less so, but if you serve with plenty of bread and maybe a green salad it would stretch. You can also double the amount of beans.

Heat your pressure cooker and add the oil. When hot, add the chorizo, onion and pepper and sauté together until the chorizo has rendered out plenty of ochre-coloured oil and has browned. Pour in the tomatoes, rinse out the can with 100ml (3½fl oz) of water and add this too, along with the beans and vinegar. Season with salt and pepper.

Stir to make sure the base of the cooker is completely deglazed, then close the lid and bring up to high pressure. Adjust the heat so it is just high enough to maintain the pressure and cook for 5 minutes. Fast release.

Make 4 wells in the beans and crack in the eggs. Sprinkle with the cheese and close the lid. Bring up to pressure again, then remove from the heat and leave for 1 minute. Fast release the rest of the pressure and leave to keep warm in the residual heat for a few minutes.

If you are making the sauce, put everything in a small food processor with a generous pinch of salt and pepper. Blitz until you have a bright green sauce. Portion the eggs and beans into bowls and drizzle the sauce over the eggs to serve.

SPICE

I first started using pressure cookers in a serious way around the time I persuaded my South Asian mother-in-law to show me her family's favourite recipes. She wasn't keen on pressure cookers, despite their popularity in Karachi, where she grew up. So I adapted her recipes for pressure cooking and realized immediately that it was brilliant for tenderizing all the lamb and mutton dishes we loved, but also – and this was a revelation – that I actually preferred the intensified, deeper flavours of the pressure-cooked food. Flavours that can sometimes disappear – such as curry leaf, so aromatic, yet often elusive – enter the heart of whatever they are cooked with, be it meat, vegetables or grain. Over time, this made me modify the amount of spice I use – for example, I cut down on the Scotch bonnet used in my Caribbean curries because pressure cooking was almost too effective at pushing the heat into everything.

Most of the dishes in this chapter have mild to moderate heat because I want them to be family friendly. If you make a dish fairly mild and serve hotter condiments or sliced chillies at the table everyone is happy. I suggest cooking the recipes as given the first time you make them – just keep a note to add more heat next time round if necessary.

AN ADAPTABLE CHICKEN CURRY

Serves 4

2 tbsp olive or vegetable oil

1 large onion, finely sliced

4 garlic cloves, crushed

15g (½oz) piece of ginger, grated (minced)

1 bunch of coriander (cilantro), stems and leaves finely chopped separately

1 tsp ground turmeric

1 tsp cayenne

½ tsp ground cinnamon

8 bone-in, skinless chicken thighs

200g (7oz) tomatoes, preferably fresh, puréed

100ml (3½fl oz) yogurt or kefir

Sea salt and freshly ground black pepper

FOR THE WHOLE SPICES
(or use 1 tablespoon of curry powder instead)

1 tsp mustard seeds

1 tsp cumin seeds

2 cloves

4 black cardamom pods

TO FINISH (OPTIONAL)

A sprinkle of garam masala

Green chillies, finely chopped

This is one of my mother-in-law's curries from my *Chicken* book, which I have adapted a bit as my tastes have changed. It is quick enough to do on a Friday night when you are tired and would otherwise be reaching for a takeaway menu. It also gives quite a lot of gravy so it is a good one to double carbs with: rice AND flatbread. And perhaps a dry vegetable curry on the side.

If you have made the Onion, Garlic and Ginger Paste on page 240, use 4 tablespoons or cubes of this in place of the fresh equivalent listed here. Any of the spices, including the whole ones, can be replaced with hot curry powder.

Heat your pressure cooker and add the oil and the whole spices. When they start popping, stir in the onion and sauté for a couple of minutes before adding the garlic, ginger, 2 tablespoons of the chopped coriander stems and the ground spices. Stir to combine then add the chicken. Cook for a couple of minutes on each side so the chicken is coated with the spices, and season with salt and pepper.

Pour in the tomatoes and stir to make sure the base of the cooker is completely deglazed. Check that plenty of steam is being generated and close the lid. (Resist any temptation to add water at this stage; as long as you have deglazed properly there should not be a problem as there is plenty of water in the onion and chicken).

Bring up to high pressure and adjust the heat so it is just high enough to maintain the pressure. Cook for 10 minutes, then remove from the heat and leave to drop pressure naturally.

Stir in the yogurt and sprinkle over the garam masala (if using). Leave to stand for a few minutes over a very low heat – you will find the sauce thickens up a little to a rich gravy. Stir in the coriander leaves at the last minute and serve with green chillies, if you like, for extra heat.

LAMB AND SPINACH CURRY

Serves 4-6

1 tbsp coconut oil

2 cloves

5 black cardamom pods

½ cinnamon stick

12 curry leaves (optional)

1 onion, thickly sliced

2 tbsp curry powder or use the basic spice mix (see page 241)

4 garlic cloves, crushed or grated

Stems from 1 small bunch of coriander (cilantro), finely chopped, plus a few whole sprigs to serve (optional)

15g (½oz) piece of ginger, grated (minced)

800g (1lb 12oz) lamb neck fillet, trimmed and cut into large chunks

2 medium potatoes, cut into chunks slightly larger than the lamb

750g (1lb 10oz) frozen whole-leaf spinach, preferably defrosted

Juice of 1 lemon

Sea salt and freshly ground black pepper

A few sliced green chillies, to serve

When I was writing this book, I did a few polls on favourite recipes and of all the lamb curries, a lamb/mutton/goat saag came out on top. This was pleasing – it is a go-to in our house as I pretty much always have frozen spinach in the freezer. Of course, it can be made with fresh spinach if you prefer, but it will need cooking down first so the amount of liquid given out doesn't flood the curry.

Pressure cooking lamb and spinach together gives you that soft, thick, oleaginous quality I associate with very long cooking – it is very moreish. When I can get it, I also like adding some fenugreek leaf (fresh or frozen).

You can serve this with rice or flatbreads and maybe a dal/lentil curry. Try the one on page 81.

Heat your pressure cooker and add the coconut oil, the whole spices and curry leaves, if using. When the spice aroma hits you and/or the curry leaves start to crackle and pop, add the onion, curry powder or spice mix, garlic, coriander stems and ginger. Stir to combine for a couple of minutes, then add the lamb and potatoes and season with plenty of salt. Pour over 100ml (3½fl oz) of water and stir to make sure the base of the cooker is completely deglazed. Squeeze the excess water from the defrosted spinach and add to the cooker. Alternatively, put the frozen spinach on top if you haven't had time to defrost.

Bring up to high pressure, then adjust the heat until it is just high enough to maintain the pressure. Cook for 15 minutes. Remove from the heat and leave to drop pressure naturally. Taste for seasoning and add a little lemon juice. If you used still-frozen spinach, you might want to reduce the liquid levels a little, so leave to simmer for a few minutes. Regardless, leave to stand for a few minutes, then garnish with sprigs of coriander, if you like, and serve with green chillies.

PEPPER BEEF

Serves 4-6

2 tbsp olive oil or beef dripping if you have it

1kg (2lb 4oz) beef shin, trimmed and cut into large chunks

1 head of garlic, cloves pierced with a knife tip

3 bay leaves

1 tbsp coarsely ground black pepper

1 tbsp coarsely ground white pepper

1 tsp sea salt

Enough red wine to cover

As a food writer, constantly surrounded by a wide variety of ingredients, it can be hard to remember that sometimes less is more, which is why I always like coming across recipes that are deliberately minimalist and don't feel as though something is missing. This classic Tuscan beef dish – peposo – is one of those. It is normally served with bread, but I like it with a big pile of buttered cavolo nero. Leftovers can be cut up and stirred through pasta for a peppery ragù.

I use beef shin in this recipe because the connective tissue dissolves into the wine and gives body to the cooking liquor, but you can also use stewing or braising steak – reduce the cook time at high pressure to just 20 minutes.

Heat your pressure cooker and add half the oil or dripping. When hot, sear the beef in batches, making sure you don't crowd them (you want them to sear, not steam) adding more oil or fat as necessary. Return all the beef to the cooker, along with any juices. Add the garlic, bay leaves, the two peppers and the salt. Pour over the red wine. Stir to make sure the base of the cooker is completely deglazed.

Close the lid and bring up to high pressure. Adjust the heat until it is just high enough to maintain the pressure, cook for 45 minutes, then remove from the heat and leave to drop pressure naturally.

Scoop out the garlic cloves and squeeze their flesh into the sauce. Taste and adjust the seasoning, including more black pepper if you think it needs it.

The sauce will probably look very runny (traditionally it is supposed to be) but it will thicken up a little as it cools. Serve immediately or, even better, reheat the following day.

SPICED COCONUT AND SWEETCORN CHICKEN

Serves 4

300g (10½oz) sweetcorn (frozen is ideal, or fresh cut from cobs)

1 tbsp coconut oil

400g (14oz) chicken thigh fillets, roughly chopped

3 tbsp Thai red curry paste – bought or see page 242

400ml (14fl oz) can coconut milk

400ml (14oz) fish, chicken or vegetable stock

2 tbsp fish sauce

1 tsp palm or soft light brown sugar

6 makrut lime leaves, shredded

1 red (bell) pepper, cut into strips

200g (7oz) squash or pumpkin, diced

Juice of 1 lime

100g (3½oz) fresh spinach

300g (10½oz) raw, peeled king prawns (jumbo shrimp)

TO SERVE

Rice (try the Sesame Rice on page 207)

1 small bunch of coriander (cilantro), finely chopped

1 small bunch of Thai basil, leaves picked

Sliced chillies

Chilli oil (optional)

This dish is very fast to put together, even if you make your own paste rather than using shop bought. If you do buy a paste, it is up to you what sort but red curry paste would work well.

Put 100g (3½oz) of the sweetcorn in a food processor and blitz – it will give a bit of texture to the cooking liquid.

Heat your pressure cooker and add the oil. When it has melted, add the chicken and stir briefly to colour. Add 2 tablespoons of the paste, along with the blitzed sweetcorn, coconut milk, stock, fish sauce, sugar and lime leaves. Stir, then add the remaining sweetcorn, red pepper and squash. Bring up to high pressure and immediately remove from the heat. Leave to drop pressure naturally.

Remove the lid, stir in the lime juice and taste – it may need the remaining paste or more fish sauce. Push the spinach into the sauce, followed by the prawns. Leave over a low heat until the prawns are cooked through.

Serve over rice garnished with the coriander, Thai basil and chillies for extra heat. You can also serve with a chilli oil at the table.

A SIMPLE DAL

Serves 4

1 tbsp coconut oil

A handful of curry leaves (optional)

1 large onion, finely chopped

6 garlic cloves, crushed

15g (½oz) piece of ginger, crushed

1 tbsp curry powder or use the basic spice mix (see page 241)

200g (7oz) dried whole red, brown or green lentils, rinsed

200g (7oz) tomatoes, canned or fresh, puréed

400ml (14fl oz) can coconut milk

1 tsp garam masala

Sea salt and freshly ground black pepper

TO GARNISH

Coriander (cilantro), chopped

Green chillies, sliced

Most of the dal recipes I make use split lentils, which generally break down into the liquid, but sometimes a whole version – in which the lentils remain intact – can be really good. I played around with this a lot when given some British-grown red lentils to try but it works just as well with any brown or green whole lentils you can buy.

Again, if you have any Onion, Garlic and Ginger Paste made up (see page 240), you can use some of that in place of the fresh ingredients here.

Heat your pressure cooker and add the oil and the curry leaves, if using. Wait for them to crackle before adding the onion. Sauté until a light golden brown then add the garlic and ginger and cook for another couple of minutes. Stir in the curry powder or spices and the lentils and stir to combine. Pour in the tomatoes and coconut milk, followed by 600ml (21fl oz) of water. Season generously – lentils will take a lot of salt. Stir to make sure the base of the pan is completely deglazed.

Close the lid and bring up to high pressure, then adjust the heat so it is just high enough to maintain the pressure. Cook for 7 minutes, then remove from the heat and leave to drop pressure naturally. Stir in the garam masala and taste for seasoning.

Serve garnished with coriander and green chillies for extra heat.

SOY AND GINGER PORK

Serves 4

750g (1b 10oz) diced pork meat
(shoulder is good but any is fine)

75ml (2¼fl oz) malt vinegar

15g (½oz) piece of ginger, peeled

2 tbsp olive oil

4 onions, quartered, or 8 shallots,
halved lengthways

1 tbsp light soft brown sugar

1 tbsp light soy sauce

1 tbsp dark soy sauce

Sea salt and freshly ground
black pepper

Steamed rice, to serve

OPTIONAL EXTRA

Your choice of greens, such as
pak choi

This is a recipe based on a curry from MiMi Aye's cookbook *Mandalay*, a fascinating exploration of Burmese food. I have taken liberties a bit, especially with the method, but the first step of tossing the pork in vinegar gives absolutely wondrous results in terms of flavour. It is a bit like 'washing' meat in lime juice, which is something I learned to do in the Caribbean, and gives the same savoury intensity.

Put the pork in a bowl and pour over the vinegar. Toss to make sure all pieces are coated, then drain. Put in your pressure cooker and add just enough water to almost cover the pork. Season with plenty of salt and pepper. Bring to high pressure then adjust the heat until it is just high enough to maintain the pressure. Cook for 10 minutes, then remove from the heat and leave to drop pressure naturally. Remove the pork from the pressure cooker, reserving the cooking liquor, and set aside.

Put the ginger in a small food processor with 2 tablespoons of the cooking liquor and blitz to a sauce. Alternatively, pound the ginger to a paste using a pestle and mortar, adding the same amount of cooking liquor. Strain and discard the solids.

Wipe out your pressure cooker, reheat and add the oil. When hot, place the onions or shallots, cut side down, in the oil and sear on all sides – you want a decent bit of colour here. Push to one side and return the pork. Let it sear briefly, but be careful not to break it up too much. Add the ginger paste and all the remaining ingredients and stir to combine. Add 200ml (7fl oz) of the cooking liquor and stir to make sure the base of the cooker is completely deglazed.

Close the lid and bring up to high pressure again and cook for 5 minutes. Remove from the heat and leave to drop pressure naturally.

At this point you can add greens to the cooker – bring up to high pressure again and do zero minutes, fast release. Serve with steamed rice.

RIBS IN GINGER BEER

Serves 4

1kg (2lb 4oz) fat pork ribs

1 tsp allspice berries, lightly crushed

6 garlic cloves, crushed

15g (½in) piece of ginger, grated (minced)

2 tbsp Pickapeppa sauce OR HP sauce

1 Scotch bonnet, left whole (optional)

500ml (17fl oz) ginger beer

1 large sprig thyme

2 bay leaves

Sea salt and freshly ground black pepper

I don't think it is possible for me to write a pressure cooker book without including a pork rib recipe – this will be my third and this time I am inspired by some of my favourite Caribbean flavours.

I think a really fiery ginger beer is necessary, but I take a belt and braces approach here and add fresh root too. Plus a Scotch bonnet, which I have made optional as it does pack a punch. You could use a milder chilli instead, if you prefer, or just omit.

Put everything in your pressure cooker – no need to brown the ribs, especially if you are grilling or frying them after pressure cooking. Season with plenty of salt and pepper.

Close the lid and bring up to high pressure, then adjust the heat until it is just high enough to maintain the pressure. Cook at high pressure for 30 minutes for tender ribs, 45 minutes if you want them falling off the bone. Remove from the heat and leave to drop pressure naturally.

Remove the lid and carefully remove the ribs. Bring the remaining liquor to the boil and reduce to a syrupy sauce. Strain and return it to the cooker. Add the ribs and heat through again – the sauce should caramelize around the ribs a little. Alternatively, you can fry, grill or barbecue the ribs if you prefer, using the sauce as a glaze.

LEFTOVERS

If in the rare event of you having leftovers, pull the meat off the bones. I add to pressure-cooked fried rice or noodle dishes along with any of the leftover liquor. You don't need much per portion for the flavour to be carried through.

CARIBBEAN SEAFOOD CURRY

Serves 4

1 tbsp coconut oil

1 onion, thickly sliced

500g (1lb 2oz) squid tubes, cut into rings and patted dry

3 garlic cloves, finely chopped

1 tsp ground allspice

½ tsp ground cinnamon

1 large sprig of thyme

1 large white sweet potato, peeled and cut into chunks

1 Scotch bonnet, left whole, pierced with a knife tip

400ml (14fl oz) can coconut milk

100g (3½oz) fresh baby leaf spinach

Juice of ½ lime

Sea salt and freshly ground black pepper

FOR THE FISH

Zest and juice of 1 lime

1 garlic clove, grated (minced)

500g (1lb 2oz) white fish fillets, cut into chunks

200g (7oz) shelled prawns (shrimp) (optional)

FOR THE SALSA (OPTIONAL)

1 mango, finely diced

100g (3½oz) cherry tomatoes, diced

½ Scotch bonnet, very finely diced

Zest and juice of 1 lime

1 small red onion, finely diced

Pinch of ground allspice

If I were in the Caribbean, I would use conch for this, but squid has a similar, albeit softer, texture and is a good substitute. It is also relatively cheap and it works surprisingly well in spiced dishes.

Purple-skinned, white-fleshed sweet potatoes are now available in most supermarkets – they have a nutty flavour and firm texture. You can substitute with regular potatoes or a firm-fleshed pumpkin, but avoid orange sweet potato as they will disintegrate as they cook.

The marinade is my take on the process of 'washing' meat or seafood in lime juice – it intensifies the savoury qualities of the fish.

I serve this with the Cheat Rice and Peas on page 209.

Heat your pressure cooker and add the oil. When it has melted, add the onion and squid rings. Sauté until the base of the cooker looks dry – it is likely some liquid will come out of the squid and you don't want this flooding your gravy.

Stir in the garlic and spices, then add the thyme, sweet potato and Scotch bonnet. Pour over the coconut milk and season with salt and pepper. Stir to deglaze the pan.

Close the lid and bring up to high pressure. Adjust the heat so it is just high enough to maintain the pressure, then cook for 5 minutes. Remove from the heat and leave to drop pressure naturally.

For the fish, put the lime zest and juice into a bowl with the garlic, a generous pinch of salt and 300ml (10½fl oz) of water. Add the fish and prawns, if using. Toss to coat and leave to stand while the squid cooks.

For the salsa, mix everything together and season with salt and pepper.

When the cooker has dropped pressure, remove the lid. Drain the fish and add to the cooker. Put handfuls of the spinach over the top, making sure it doesn't touch the sides. Close the lid, bring it up to low pressure, immediately remove from the heat and leave to stand for 1 minute before opening.

Stir the spinach very gently into the coconut gravy and add the lime juice. Check for seasoning, then serve with the salsa, if using.

HALLOUMI WITH SOUR ORANGE, CHILLI AND CORIANDER

Serves 4

FOR THE SAUCE

8 garlic cloves

1 large bunch of coriander (cilantro) (around 100g/3½oz), roughly chopped

1–2 chilli peppers, depending on sort and how hot you want it (I usually use 1 Scotch bonnet)

Zest of 1 Seville orange or lime

250ml (8¾fl oz) sour orange juice OR 200ml (7fl oz) sweet orange juice and 50ml (1¾oz) lime juice

1 tbsp olive oil

FOR THE HALLOUMI

2 tbsp olive oil

1–2 x 200g (7oz) blocks halloumi, sliced (depending on appetite)

2 red onions, sliced into slim wedges

750g waxy potatoes, sliced

500g frozen peas

The hot/sour flavour combination of this sauce is one I revisit every year. My first pressure cooker book has a version made with lamb, but I was looking for a faster and cheaper option and the halloumi works really well. The potatoes make the dish one-pot and the peas cook down to a soft sweetness which complements the other flavours perfectly. The peas do lose their brightness but this is exactly how they should be.

When Seville oranges are in season, I make a lot of this sauce and freeze it, but you can use a combination of sweet orange and lime juice for a similar sweet/sour flavour when they are not.

First make the sauce. Do this in 2 stages. First, finely chop the garlic, coriander, chillies and zest together (by hand or in a food processor), then remove a few spoonfuls to use as a gremolata to finish off the dish at the end. Then, add a little water to what you have left and continue to chop or process to a purée. Mix in the sour orange juice and olive oil.

If you want to brown your halloumi (entirely optional), heat 1 tablespoon of the oil in a frying pan and sear the halloumi on both sides. Remove from the frying pan and set aside.

Heat your pressure cooker and add the remaining oil. Add the red onions and sear briefly on each side, then stir in the potatoes and peas. Pour the sauce over the contents of your pressure cooker. Stir to make sure the base is deglazed and add 100ml (3½fl oz) of water. Season with salt and pepper.

Arrange the halloumi on top and close the lid. Bring up to high pressure then adjust the heat so it is just high enough to maintain the pressure. Cook for 5 minutes, then leave to drop pressure naturally. This is slightly longer than is usually needed for potatoes, but the sauce needs the cooking time to mellow a bit.

Sprinkle over the reserved gremolata before serving.

KOREAN-INSPIRED GINGER VEGETABLES

Serves 4

200g (7oz) chard

1 tbsp olive oil

1 small onion or shallot, finely chopped

500g (1lb 2oz) pumpkin or squash, cut into large chunks (no need to peel if you don't want to)

250g (9oz) cooked black beans (see page 231 for the cooking instructions)

2 tbsp finely chopped coriander (cilantro) stems, plus extra whole sprigs to serve

Sea salt and freshly ground black pepper

FOR THE SAUCE

1 tbsp gochujang

15g (½oz) piece of ginger, grated (minced)

3 garlic cloves, crushed or grated (minced)

2 tsp maple syrup

2 tbsp dark soy sauce

TO SERVE

1 tsp black sesame seeds

A few drops of toasted sesame oil

This came about one evening when I wanted to make something fiery and realized I had some gochujang to use up. Once you have made the sauce – which takes only moments – it is very easy to put together. I would serve it with the Sesame Rice on page 207. My children like it with tacos... and they might even add cheese too.

The short cooking time here is very forgiving to the tender flesh of squash and pumpkin, but if you can use a relatively firm-fleshed one, such as crown prince, so much the better.

First make the sauce by mixing all the ingredients together and adding 150ml (5fl oz) of water.

Separate the chard leaves from the stems. Finely slice the stems and roughly tear the leaves.

Heat your pressure cooker and add the oil. When hot, add the onion and chard stems. Sauté for a couple of minutes, then stir in the pumpkin or squash, followed by the black beans and coriander stems. Season with a little salt and pepper.

Pour in the sauce and stir to make sure the base is completely deglazed. Add the chard leaves, then close the lid and bring up to high pressure. Adjust the heat so it is just high enough to maintain the pressure, cook for 2 minutes, then fast release.

Carefully stir so everything is well combined but make sure you don't break up the pumpkin or squash. Serve with a few sprigs of coriander, a sprinkling of sesame seeds and a few drops of toasted sesame oil.

BEETROOT AND PANEER CURRY

Serves 4

2 tbsp coconut or olive oil

20 curry leaves (optional)

1 tsp mustard seeds

1 large onion, very finely chopped

4 garlic cloves, crushed or grated (minced)

15g (½oz) piece of ginger, grated (minced)

1½ tbsp curry powder or use the basic spice mix (see page 241)

200g (7oz) tomatoes, fresh or canned, puréed

400g (14oz) cooked beetroot, cut into wedges (see page 201 for cooking instructions)

250g (9oz) paneer, cut into 2cm (¾in) dice

100g (3½oz) fresh or frozen spinach

Sea salt and freshly ground black pepper

TO GARNISH

Green chillies, finely chopped

A few sprigs of coriander (cilantro), chopped

Lemon wedges

This was the surprise hit during the summer of 2023, cooked several times when large bunches of beetroots were available for pence at the farmers' market. It is fresh and warming at the same time, perfect on its own for a light lunch with some flatbread. You can get away with using vacuum-packed beetroot in this recipe, but I would strongly recommend buying raw beetroot and cooking it yourself. Not only will you have more control over the texture (I can't be the only one who finds vacuum-packed beetroot a bit on the soft side) but you get the leaves as an extra green.

The curry leaves aren't essential here, but the pressure cooker does a very good job of pushing their flavour into the other ingredients so they are worth using, if you can get hold of them. Most supermarkets sell small packets of them. It is my ambition to keep a healthy curry leaf tree growing, but I am not having much success so far.

Heat your pressure cooker and add the oil. When hot, add the curry leaves (if using) and mustard seeds. Wait until you can hear them crackle and pop, then add the onion. Sauté until a light golden brown, then stir in the garlic, ginger and curry powder or spice mix and stir for a further 2 minutes.

Add the tomatoes with 100ml (3½fl oz) of water and season with salt and pepper. Stir to deglaze the pan, close the lid and bring up to high pressure. Adjust the heat so it is just high enough to maintain the pressure and cook for 5 minutes, then fast release.

Remove the lid and add the beetroot and paneer to the sauce, then place the spinach on top. Close the lid and bring up to high pressure again. Immediately remove from the heat and leave to drop pressure naturally. Open and stir.

Serve with green chillies for extra heat, a little coriander and lemon wedges to squeeze over.

SPICED COCONUT PRAWNS

Serves 4

400ml (14fl oz) coconut milk

3 tbsp curry paste (shop-bought or use the green curry paste on page 242)

300ml (10½fl oz) fish, chicken or vegetable stock

2 tbsp fish sauce

1 tsp palm or soft light brown sugar

6 makrut lime leaves, shredded

1 red (bell) pepper, cut into strips

150g (5½oz) baby corn

200g (7oz) green beans, trimmed

Zest and juice of 1 lime

3 spring onions, finely sliced

300g (10½oz) raw, peeled king prawns

Sea salt and freshly ground black pepper

TO SERVE

Sesame Rice (see page 207), optional

1 small bunch of coriander (cilantro) and/or Thai basil

Sliced chillies

Chilli oil (optional)

You will be amazed at how quickly this dish comes together once you have assembled the ingredients – it makes for a very easy weeknight dinner. However, if you ever buy prawns with the heads and tails attached, it is no effort whatsoever to turn them into a stock and it will really pay dividends. Simply toast them first in your pressure cooker, add the stock and bring up to high pressure. Leave to drop pressure naturally, then strain and use in the recipe. That's all you need to do. You can also make it much more substantial by adding more seafood.

Set your pressure cooker over a low heat and add the coconut milk and paste. Stir to combine, then add the stock, fish sauce and sugar. Stir until the sugar has dissolved, then add the lime leaves, red pepper, baby corn and green beans. Season with salt and pepper.

Close the lid and bring up to high pressure. Immediately remove from the heat and leave to stand for 1 minute. Fast release the remaining pressure.

Stir in the lime zest and juice and taste – add more fish sauce if necessary. Add the spring onions and prawns and leave on a very low heat until they are just cooked through.

Serve in bowls as is, or over rice, garnished with chopped coriander, Thai basil and chillies for extra heat. You can also serve with chilli oil at the table.

SAUSAGE AND EGG CURRY

Serves 4

4 sausages, any sort

2 tbsp olive oil

1 onion, finely sliced

4 cloves garlic

2 tbsp curry powder or use the basic spice mix (see page 241)

3 tbsp tomato purée

100g (3½oz) red lentils, rinsed

4 eggs

Sea salt and freshly ground black pepper

TO SERVE

100g (3½oz) cheese (optional)

Warm flatbreads (optional)

A few sprigs of coriander (cilantro), chopped

Sliced chillies

This is a recipe which came about from necessity (not much in the house to eat) and was so beloved it became part of the regular repertoire. It's quite economical because you don't need much meat or egg and you can substitute either with more vegetables if you want to. Things I have added include a few mushrooms in place of the sausages, stirring in the same way, or a few cubes of frozen spinach after deglazing.

Cut each sausage casing lengthways to remove, then divide the sausagemeat into 3 balls.

Heat your pressure cooker and add the oil. When hot, add the sausage balls and sear briefly on all sides. Remove and set aside.

Add the onion to the pressure cooker and stir to help deglaze the base. After 2–3 minutes, add the garlic and curry powder. Stir for a minute then add the tomato purée and lentils. Pour in 250ml (9fl oz) of water and stir to make sure the base of the cooker is completely deglazed. Season with salt and pepper.

Return the sausages to the cooker. Place a trivet and steamer basket on top and put the eggs in the basket.

Bring up to high pressure and adjust the heat so it is just high enough to maintain the pressure. Cook for 3 minutes, then remove from the heat and leave to drop pressure naturally for 3 minutes, then fast release any remaining pressure.

Remove the eggs from the basket and remove the trivet from the cooker. Plunge the eggs into cold water and peel when cool enough to handle. Cut in half lengthways.

Stir the contents of the pressure cooker and drop in the eggs, cut side up. Sprinkle with cheese, if using, then place the lid loosely on top and leave for a few minutes on a gentle heat to melt the cheese.

Serve with flatbreads, a sprinkling of coriander and a few sliced chillies for heat.

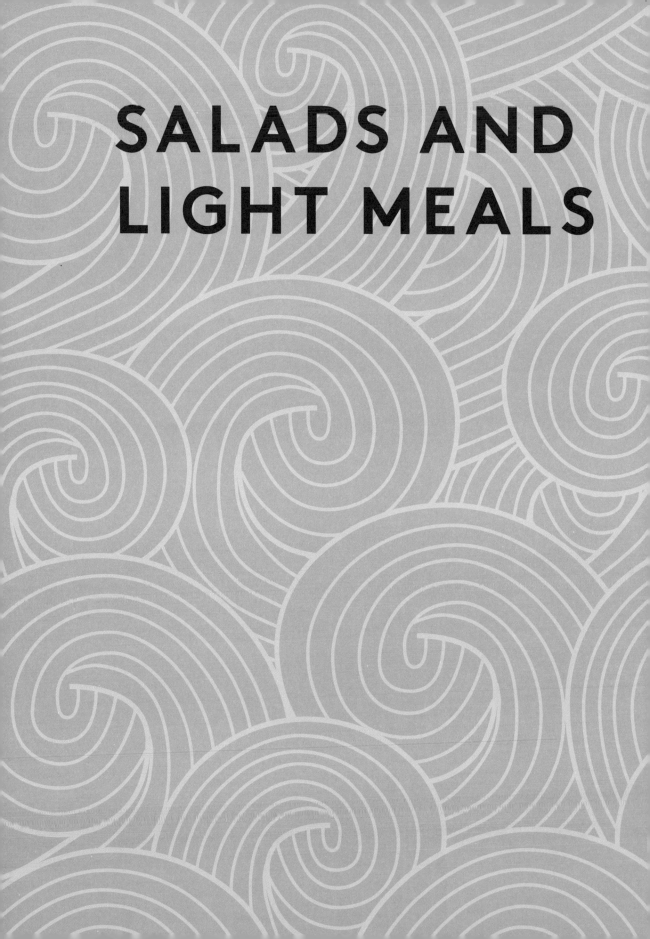

SALADS AND LIGHT MEALS

One of the assumptions many people make about pressure cookers is that they are mainly for cold-weather meals – the soups, stews and casseroles we want in the winter months. This, I think, is partly an issue with perception, but also perhaps because people don't understand quite how good pressure cookers are at cooking single ingredients as well as one-pot dishes.

The truth is that these cookers are just as useful in summer – in some ways more so, because if you cook in a pressure cooker, you are relying less on your oven and hob and that means a cooler kitchen.

If you eat a lot of salads or lightly cooked greens in summer, the pressure cooker is definitely your friend. Think how many salads have a cooked element – salad potatoes, roasted or steamed vegetables, grains, pastas, beans, pulses, meats... you can pressure cook all of these and keep them in the fridge ready for you to pull a salad together quickly. And if you end up cooking several things at once, as I suggest in some of these recipes, you are really winning in terms of saving on energy bills too.

ORZO AND CHICKEN SALAD

Serves 4

1 tbsp olive oil

1 small onion, finely chopped

100g (3½oz) orzo

½ tsp ground ginger

¼ tsp ground cinnamon

2 sprigs of thyme

4 skinless chicken thigh fillets

150g (5½oz) green beans, topped and tailed, or runner beans, trimmed and sliced

200g (7oz) watercress

100g (3½oz) red or black grapes, halved

Sea salt and freshly ground black pepper

FOR THE DRESSING

2 tbsp olive oil

Zest and juice of ½ lemon

½ tsp honey

1 garlic clove, halved

TO FINISH

50g (1¾oz) flaked almonds, toasted

A few mint and parsley leaves

I love pasta cooked with spices. I once had a very memorable meal in southeast France which was simply baked pasta with ginger, served with a small roast chicken, and it has stayed with me ever since. The combination was the inspiration for this salad.

First make the salad dressing. Whisk everything together and season with salt and pepper. Set aside, giving the garlic time to infuse, until you are ready to dress the salad.

Heat your pressure cooker and add the oil. When hot, add the onion and orzo and toast for 3–4 minutes until the orzo starts to colour. Stir in the spices and pour over 200ml (7fl oz) of water. Season with salt and pepper.

Drop in one of the thyme sprigs, put in the chicken thighs, season and add the other thyme sprig. Wrap the beans in foil and place on top of the chicken.

Close the lid and bring up to high pressure. Adjust the heat so it is just high enough to maintain the pressure, then cook for 5 minutes. Fast release, off the heat.

Remove the beans and chicken from the cooker and discard the thyme. Give the orzo a quick stir – it will be quite sticky at this point, but leave to cool and the grains will soon separate. Shred the chicken.

Assemble the salad. Arrange the watercress and beans over a platter. Fork through the orzo to separate the grains, then sprinkle it over. Add the chicken and grapes, then drizzle over the salad dressing, discarding the garlic. Finish with the almonds, mint and parsley.

ROAST RED PEPPER AND 'NDUJA SALAD

Serves 4

1 small red onion, finely sliced

2 tbsp olive oil

75g (2½oz) pearled spelt (optional), rinsed

4 red (bell) peppers, halved and deseeded

150g (5½oz) rocket (arugula) or similar salad leaves

150g (5½oz) cherry tomatoes, halved

2 tbsp capers

Leaves from a bunch of flat-leaf parsley, chopped

Sea salt and freshly ground black pepper

FOR THE DRESSING

1 tbsp olive oil

50g (1¾oz) 'nduja, crumbled

1 tbsp sherry vinegar

Zest and juice of ½ lemon

½ tsp dried thyme

This is a bit of a deconstructed Diana Henry recipe. The 'roast' peppers with the 'nduja dressing are great on their own, with just some bread, but I have turned it into a salad. I've included a grain, but don't feel tied to this. A pile of Puy lentils would work equally well, as would serving with bread on the side.

First sprinkle the red onion with 1 teaspoon of salt and cover with cold water. Leave for 30 minutes, then drain.

Cook the spelt (if using). Heat your pressure cooker and add 1 tablespoon of the oil. When hot, add the spelt and sauté for a couple of minutes to lightly toast, then add 225ml (7¾fl oz) of water. Season generously and close the lid. Bring up to high pressure and adjust the heat to just high enough to maintain the pressure. Cook for 12 minutes, then remove from the heat and allow to drop pressure naturally. Leave to cool then transfer to a bowl. Clean the cooker to cook the peppers.

Heat your pressure cooker again, add the remaining tablespoon of oil and put in the peppers, cut side down. Cook for a couple of minutes, then flip over and cook for another 3–4 minutes until starting to char. Add a splash of water and close the lid. Bring up to high pressure and cook for 1 minute, then remove from the heat and allow to drop pressure naturally. Remove from the cooker and set aside, covered, to cool to room temperature. Peel and pull intro strips.

To make the dressing, heat the oil in the pan and when hot, and stir in the 'nduja. When it has pretty much dissolved, remove from the heat and whisk in the vinegar, lemon zest and juice and thyme. Season and taste, adjusting the salt, pepper and lemon as necessary.

To assemble, distribute the spelt over a platter or in individual salad bowls and toss with the salad leaves. Arrange the strips of pepper over the top, along with the drained onion, tomatoes and capers. Drizzle with dressing and sprinkle with the parsley. Serve at room temperature.

GADO GADO

Serves 4

250g (9oz) salad potatoes, thickly sliced

4 eggs

200g (7oz) green beans, trimmed

100g (3½oz) baby corn, halved lengthways

½ Chinese leaf (Napa cabbage), finely shredded

1 carrot, julienned

½ cucumber, sliced

100g (3½oz) cherry tomatoes, halved

50g (1¾oz) radishes, sliced

1 handful of coriander (cilantro), mint and Thai basil leaves (at least two herbs)

A few drops of toasted sesame oil

Sea salt

FOR THE DRESSING

100g (3½oz) crunchy peanut butter

1 tbsp fish sauce

1 tbsp hot sauce

1 tsp soft light brown sugar or honey

1 garlic clove, crushed

5g (⅛oz) piece of ginger, grated (minced)

1 tbsp tamarind paste (optional)

Juice of 1 limes

The method below really makes a difference to how quickly you can get this meal onto the table. Before I started pressure cooking, a lazy day would have me avoiding a salad like this, purely because of the need to cook the various elements separately. However, gado gado is a dish I love (as do the family – it's the peanut butter), so I had to work out if everything could be cooked together. So much time- and fuel-saving! After that, it is just an assembly job.

Gado gado is often served with tofu or seitan, so you can add either of these or swap out the eggs, if you prefer.

First, the cooking part. Pour 2cm (¾in) of water into your pressure cooker. Add the sliced potatoes and season with salt. Place a trivet and steamer basket on top and put the eggs in the basket. Take a piece of foil, arrange the green beans and corn on it, and season with salt. Bring the sides of the foil up around the vegetables but do not seal as a parcel – you want it open at the top so it looks a bit like a galette – and place on top of the eggs.

Close the lid and bring up to pressure. Adjust the heat so it is just enough to maintain the pressure and cook for 3 minutes. Remove from the heat and fast release.

Cool the potatoes, eggs and vegetables under cold running water, then toss in the sesame oil. Prepare the remaining salad ingredients.

Make the dressing by whisking all the ingredients together. Taste and add salt as necessary. You might also want more of any of the other ingredients: getting the balance of sweet/salt/sour/hot is very much down to individual taste. If it seems too thick, add a little water – just a tablespoon at a time.

Assemble the salad, either on a large platter or in individual bowls – I present it buddha bowl-style. Start with the shredded Chinese leaf, followed by the potatoes and arrange the eggs and remaining ingredients around them. Drizzle over most of the dressing and serve the rest at the table for adding during the meal.

EGG, LENTIL AND TUNA SALAD

Serves 4

100g (3½oz) brown, green or Puy lentils, rinsed

1 tsp olive oil

4–6 eggs

4 garlic cloves, unpeeled

4 large handfuls of salad leaves

200g (7oz) cherry tomatoes

1 courgette (zucchini), very finely sliced (use a mandolin, if you have one)

120g (4¼oz) canned or jarred tuna (drained weight), lightly flaked

3 tbsp capers, rinsed

Handfuls of mint, basil, parsley

Sea salt and freshly ground black pepper

FOR THE DRESSING

4 tbsp olive oil

½ garlic clove, crushed

Zest of 1 lemon and juice of 2

¼ tsp chilli flakes

One of the things I love about developing recipes is figuring out how ingredients can be cooked together side by side, so I was really happy when I managed to work out this one.

I must add here that pressure cooking can be as inexact as any other method of cooking; so much depends on the type of cooker, the size and temperature of your eggs, the age of your lentils. So I have tested this with several pressure cookers to be sure.

If you find that your lentils generally take longer than 2 minutes at high pressure plus natural pressure release – and I have to say, I occasionally do – and you don't want to overcook your eggs, you can either chill the eggs first or wrap them lightly in foil. Either of these actions will slow down the cooking process.

You don't have to use canned or jarred tuna for this. You can grill fresh tuna, or sardines or mackerel if you prefer. Or mash a can of anchovies into the dressing.

Put the lentils in your pressure cooker with ½ tsp salt, 1 tsp of oil and 200ml (7fl oz) of water. Put a trivet and steamer basket into the pressure cooker and arrange the eggs and garlic cloves on top.

Close the lid, bring up to high pressure and adjust the heat to just high enough to maintain the pressure. Cook for 2 minutes, then remove from the heat and leave to drop pressure naturally. Open the cooker and remove the eggs and garlic. Run the eggs under cold water or put in a bowl of iced water before peeling. Check the lentils are cooked through – if any are a bit hard, leaving them in the cooking liquid will finish off the job as they cool. Once cool, drain and set aside.

Make the salad dressing. Whisk all the ingredients together with the flesh from the cooked garlic cloves. Season with salt and pepper.

To assemble, arrange the salad leaves, lentils, tomatoes and courgette over a platter or in individual bowls and drizzle with most of the dressing. Toss very lightly and arrange the eggs, halved or quartered, and the tuna over the top. Sprinkle with the capers and herbs and top with the remaining dressing, a little salt and some pepper.

WARM HAM AND POTATO SALAD

Serves 4

2 shallots, finely sliced

1½ tbsp cider vinegar

500g (1lb 2oz) piece of gammon (uncooked ham)

500g (1lb 2oz) salad potatoes, halved if large

1 large lettuce or equivalent in loose leaves, roughly torn

8 cornichons, sliced into rounds

A few dill fronds or flat-leaf parsley, leaves finely chopped

Sea salt and freshly ground black pepper

FOR THE DRESSING

2 tbsp olive oil

50ml (1¾fl oz) buttermilk

2 tsp cider vinegar

2 tsp wholegrain mustard

1 tbsp finely chopped tarragon leaves

½ tsp honey

This is a quick way of cooking a piece of gammon for a salad alongside the potatoes – you can then use the stock as a base for a soup.

It is up to you whether you use smoked or unsmoked gammon – just check whether it needs soaking first. Any butcher will be able to tell you this, as should the packaging on anything you might buy in the supermarket – if in doubt, ask at the meat counter.

If you do need to soak the gammon, either leave it in cold water overnight, or you can quick-soak it in the cooker. To do this, cover with cold water, close the lid and bring up to high pressure, then immediately fast release. Rinse the meat and discard the water.

Use any salad leaves you like in this, but I like to go slightly bitter and crunchy with radicchio or frisée.

Put the shallots in a small bowl and sprinkle with salt. Pour over the cider vinegar and leave for 30 minutes.

Place the gammon in your pressure cooker and almost cover with water. Put the potatoes in a steamer basket and rest it on top of the gammon.

Close the lid and bring up to high pressure. Adjust the heat so it is just high enough to maintain the pressure, then cook for 10 minutes. Remove from the heat and leave to drop pressure naturally. Remove the potatoes and ham from the cooker. As soon as the ham is cool enough to handle, pull apart into chunks.

While the ham and potatoes are cooking, make the dressing. Whisk all the ingredients together, taste and season with salt and pepper as necessary. Spoon half the dressing over the potatoes while they are still hot and leave to stand at room temperature.

To assemble the salad, arrange the lettuce leaves over a large serving platter. Add the potatoes and ham. Sprinkle the drained shallots and cornichons on top. Drizzle over more of the dressing and garnish with the dill or parsley. Serve immediately.

ROAST CABBAGE AND BACON PANZANELLA

Serves 4

1 red onion, thinly sliced

4 tbsp olive oil

1 small green pointed or red cabbage, cut into wedges

50g (1¾oz) dried cranberries

250g (9oz) stale sourdough bread, cubed

2 garlic cloves, finely chopped

1 tsp dried thyme or the leaves from a large sprig

150g (5½oz) ripe tomatoes, roughly chopped

100g (3½oz) radishes, sliced into rounds

100g (3½oz) baby leaf spinach

Sea salt and freshly ground black pepper

FOR THE DRESSING

1 tbsp olive oil

1 shallot, finely sliced

100g (3½oz) bacon lardons

2 tbsp sherry vinegar

1 tsp honey

This way of 'roasting' cabbage is one of my favourite things to do at demos, as it is so fast compared to the oven method and people are always amazed by the results. I also use the pressure cooker to soften up very stale bread – see page 246 for details. Panzanella – the Italian name for bread salad – is a fine way of using up leftover bread.

Sprinkle the red onion with salt and cover with cold water. Leave for 30 minutes.

Meanwhile cook the cabbage. Heat your pressure cooker and add 2 tablespoons of the oil. When hot, add the cabbage wedges and sear on the cut sides – you might have to do this in 2 batches so as not to crowd the pan. Allow 1–2 minutes per side to get a decent amount of colour. Sprinkle in the cranberries and season with salt and pepper. Pour in 75ml (2¼fl oz) of water. The cooker should instantly fill with steam. Put the lid on quickly and let the cooker come up to pressure. Cook for 1 minute at high pressure and fast release. Remove the contents and set aside.

To make the croûtons, heat the remaining 2 tablespoons of oil in a frying pan (skillet), add the bread and season with salt and pepper. Stir until well coated in the oil and sauté until toasted. Add the garlic and thyme and stir for a minute or two before removing from the heat. Put in a mixing bowl with the drained red onion.

Make the dressing. Heat the oil in the pan and add the shallot and bacon. Fry until both are crisp and lightly browned. Add the vinegar and honey. Swirl around the pan for a moment, then pour into the mixing bowl.

Add the cabbage (roughly chopped if the wedges are very large), cranberries, tomatoes and radishes to the bowl. Leave to stand for at least 10 minutes, then toss with the spinach. Serve at room temperature.

SQUASHED COURGETTE AND MOZZARELLA SALAD

Serves 4

3 medium courgettes (zucchini), trimmed and halved lengthways

1 tbsp olive oil

25g (1oz) Parmesan, grated

100g (3½oz) rocket (arugula) or similar salad leaves

150g (5½oz) cherry tomatoes, halved

2 balls of mozzarella, roughly torn

A few sprigs of tarragon, basil or lemon thyme, leaves finely chopped or torn

Sea salt and freshly ground black pepper

FOR THE DRESSING

3 tbsp olive oil

Zest and juice of 1 lemon

1 tbsp finely chopped tarragon leaves

2 tsp white balsamic vinegar

1 garlic clove, bruised

This is based on an Ottolenghi idea of steaming courgettes until soft then dressing them. This is much, much less hassle than sautéing or griddling - perfect for a quick late-summer salad, especially if you have a homegrown glut of courgettes and are running out of ideas.

This salad needs to be served at room temperature, so get the mozzarella out of the fridge when you start cooking the courgettes.

Put a splash of water in your pressure cooker - 100ml (3½fl oz) is plenty. Add the courgettes, skin side down. If any are too long for your cooker, halve them again. Season with salt and pepper. Close the lid and bring up to high pressure. Cook for 1 minute, then remove from the heat and leave to drop pressure naturally.

Remove the courgettes from the cooker and roughly break up - you can do this with your hands or a knife. Transfer to a colander. Cover with an up-facing plate that fits snugly on top of the courgettes and weigh down with something heavy - for example, a couple of cans. Leave to drain for around 30 minutes. Transfer to a bowl, drizzle with oil and toss through the Parmesan.

While the courgettes drain, make the dressing by whisking all the ingredients together. Season with salt and pepper, then leave so the garlic can infuse.

To assemble, arrange the salad leaves over a large platter and top with the tomatoes, courgettes and mozzarella. Drizzle over the dressing and top with the herbs.

BEETROOT, BUCKWHEAT AND SMOKED FISH SALAD

Serves 4

200g (7oz) spinach, watercress or other salad leaves

250g (9oz) cooked beetroot, cut into wedges (see page 201)

½ cucumber, diced

200g (7oz) smoked mackerel fillets, skinned and pulled into chunks

200g (7oz) ripe blackberries

50g (1¾oz) hazelnuts, lightly crushed and toasted (optional)

A few small mint leaves

Sea salt and freshly ground black pepper

FOR THE BUCKWHEAT

1 tbsp olive oil

100g (3½oz) buckwheat groats

½ tsp ground allspice

FOR THE DRESSING

1 shallot, finely chopped

50g (1¾oz) ripe blackberries

1 tbsp sherry or red wine vinegar

4 tbsp olive or hazelnut oil

1 tsp honey

2 tsp wholegrain mustard

A squeeze of lemon juice

Buckwheat is a useful grain to keep in the store cupboard. I get it out mainly for salads like this because it cooks very quickly and has a pleasant flavour which is quite versatile. It also makes a good alternative to couscous and bulgar wheat if you ever need to avoid gluten. Here I've used it in the sort of salad I like to eat in the late summer. I specify smoked mackerel in the ingredients list but I do sometime splurge on hot smoked river trout instead.

First cook the buckwheat. Heat the oil in your pressure cooker and add the buckwheat groats. Fry, stirring constantly, until the groats smell pleasantly toasted, then stir in the allspice. Season with salt and pepper, then cover with 100ml (3½fl oz) of water. Stir briefly, making sure no groats cling to the side and are pushed into the liquid.

Bring up to high pressure. Adjust the heat so it is just high enough to maintain the pressure, then cook for 3 minutes. Remove from the heat and leave to drop pressure naturally. Open the lid and fluff up the groats. Leave to cool.

To make the dressing, put the shallot in a small bowl and sprinkle with salt. Add the blackberries and roughly crush with a fork. Pour over the vinegar and leave to stand for half an hour. Whisk in the remaining ingredients and taste for seasoning – add a little more salt and some pepper if need be.

To assemble, arrange the buckwheat over a large serving platter and drizzle over some of the dressing. Add the leaves, beetroot, cucumber, and mackerel. Drizzle over most of the remaining dressing and toss very lightly. Sprinkle with the blackberries, the hazelnuts, if using, and a few mint leaves. Serve immediately.

STEAMED AUBERGINES

Serves 4

2 large aubergines (eggplants), cut into batons

2 spring onions (scallions), shredded

1 tsp black sesame seeds

Sea salt

FOR THE SAUCE

1 tbsp light soy sauce

2 tsp rice vinegar

2 tsp crushed chillies

1 garlic clove, crushed

5g (¼in) piece of ginger, grated (minced)

1 tsp toasted sesame oil

OPTIONAL EXTRAS

150g (5½oz) small mushrooms (such as enoki, button or button chestnut)

200g (7oz) kale leaves, roughly torn

About 400g (14oz) cooked rice

These were a bit of a revelation – and vanished so quickly when I served them that I had to up my quantities! Pressure-steaming aubergines results in a soft texture – juicy but not soggy. They are good as a very quick, light lunch, with or without rice, or just over some wilted greens.

It isn't strictly necessary to salt aubergines these days, if it is bitterness you are worried about. But I do find that just half an hour in a colander pays dividends in terms of umami flavour and a creamier texture.

Put the aubergines in a colander and sprinkle with 1 teaspoon of salt. If you are including mushrooms, add these too. Toss and leave to stand over a bowl for 30 minutes. Very lightly squeeze the aubergine batons – some water will come out.

Pour 2cm (¾in) of water into your pressure cooker. Add the kale, if using, along with a pinch of salt. Arrange the aubergines (and mushrooms) in a steamer basket and place on a trivet, making sure it is elevated above the water. Close the lid and bring up to high pressure. Cook for 2 minutes, then remove from the heat and leave to drop pressure naturally.

Mix all the sauce ingredients together. Taste and adjust the balance if necessary.

Strain the kale and arrange over a shallow serving bowl. Top with the aubergines (and mushrooms) and pour over the sauce. Sprinkle with the spring onions and sesame seeds. Serve as is, or with rice.

QUICK
COMFORT
FIXES

The recipes in this chapter are very much Friday night TV dinners through to Saturday teatime, the time of the week when I often don't want to put much effort into cooking because I am tired or just tearing around too much. So they mainly contain elements that can be prepared ahead for reheating or they might even have bought elements to make life easier. Embracing pressure cooking isn't about cooking everything in the pressure cooker all the time, and it certainly doesn't mean you have to cook everything from scratch all the time either.

The unifying features of these dishes are that they all have big flavours, will fill you up and will make everyone happy.

GARLIC BUTTER TOMATOES

Serves 4

1 tbsp olive oil

25g (1oz) butter

400g (14oz) cherry tomatoes

2 garlic cloves, finely chopped

Leaves from a large sprig of tarragon, finely chopped

Sea salt and freshly ground black pepper

TO SERVE

Buttered toast

Goat's cheese or curd (optional)

Summery lunch of my dreams: garlic and tarragon are absolutely the best things to put with ripe, sweet tomatoes. Here, the tomatoes cook to the point that they swell and threaten to burst, and the heat just takes the edge off the garlic. Serve with buttered toast, or spread the toast with soft goat's cheese or curd as well. (Note: as well, not instead of).

Heat up your pressure cooker and add the oil and butter. As soon as the butter has melted and started to foam, add the tomatoes and season with salt and pepper.

Pour in 50ml (1¾fl oz) of water. The cooker should instantly fill with steam. Put the lid on quickly and let the cooker come up to pressure. Remove from the heat immediately and leave to stand for 1 minute. Fast release the remaining pressure. Use a slotted spoon to transfer the tomatoes to a bowl. Add the garlic and tarragon to the cooker. Swirl around in the buttery juices for 1 minute, then pour over the tomatoes.

SPAGHETTI HOOPS

Serves 4

25g (1oz) butter

2 garlic cloves, crushed

500g (1lb 2oz) spaghetti hoops

1.2 litres (40fl oz) stock or water

400ml (14fl oz) passata

A pinch of ground cinnamon

1 onion, halved

A few sprigs of basil

Sea salt and freshly ground
black pepper

TO SERVE

Buttered toast

Grated (shredded) cheese – Cheddar
is better than Parmesan here
(optional)

Embarrassing story. Not long after my son had started school, he is at a playdate and is given Heinz spaghetti hoops for his tea. 'What is it?' he asks. 'Pasta,' he is told. 'THIS ISN'T PASTA!' he retorts. Mortification all round. There is a place for canned spaghetti – I have a bit of a fondness for many things Heinz (especially the oxtail soup), but I know what he means. This is my attempt to re-create the canned stuff in a healthier, non ultra-processed way, albeit with an al dente texture!

For some reason, spaghetti hoops take longer to cook than most other forms of pasta and also take more liquid. So if you want to use a different form, just make sure the pasta is covered, as for the other pasta recipes, and cook for 5 minutes, then fast release.

You can use stock or water here. Stock is nutritionally better, obviously, and I will use vegetable or chicken, depending on what I have available. But I also like the purity of water. The cinnamon adds sweetness, without cinnamon flavour.

Heat your pressure cooker then add the butter. When melted, add the garlic and stir for 1 minute over a low heat. Stir in the spaghetti hoops and add the stock or water. Season with plenty of salt and pepper and stir, making sure the pasta isn't sticking to the base. Quickly pour over the passata and sprinkle in the cinnamon. Place the onion halves and basil sprigs on top.

Close the lid and bring up to high pressure. Adjust the heat so it is just high enough to maintain the pressure and cook for 5 minutes, then leave to drop pressure naturally.

Fish out the onion and basil and stir thoroughly. Pile onto hot buttered toast and sprinkle with cheese if you like.

TORTILLA LASAGNE

Serves 4

1 tbsp olive oil, plus extra for greasing and for frying the tortillas (optional)

400g (14oz) minced (ground) beef

1 small red onion, diced

1 red (bell) pepper, diced

2 garlic cloves, finely chopped

2 tsp chipotle paste

1 tbsp Mexican-style spice mix (see page 241) or shop-bought equivalent (optional)

200g (7oz) canned tomatoes

250g (9oz) cooked beans – red kidney/pinto/black (see page 231 for cooking instructions)

Sea salt and freshly ground black pepper

TO ASSEMBLE

5 corn or wheat tortillas

1 small bunch of coriander (cilantro), chopped

250g (9oz) soured cream

200g (7oz) Cheddar, grated (shredded)

Pickled jalapeños or lime wedges (optional)

This is a two-step recipe, using the pressure cooker twice, but it still doesn't take long at all. If I was serving for a weekday meal, I would probably prep the sauce in advance, but it isn't inconceivable that you can do everything, from start to finish, in 50 minutes.

The meat sauce – a fast version of chilli con carne – is a good recipe in its own right so is a useful one for batch cooking. You could also use the chilli on page 132 instead. Either way, the extra time it takes is worth it for the joy it provides at table.

I might serve it with pickled jalapeños and lime wedges, but honestly, it doesn't really need a thing.

Heat your pressure cooker and add the oil. When hot, add the beef, onion and (bell) pepper. Stir over a high heat until the beef is browned, then stir in the garlic, chipotle paste and spice mix, if using. Season with salt and pepper.

Add the tomatoes and beans and stir to combine, making sure the base is completely deglazed. Close the lid and bring up to high pressure, then adjust the heat until it is just high enough to maintain the pressure. Cook for 5 minutes and fast release. Simmer to reduce if particularly watery (it shouldn't be!).

While the sauce is cooking, toast the tortillas in a lightly oiled frying pan (skillet). This step is not essential, but does give a better texture to your lasagne.

Oil and line a deep 20cm (8in) tin or ceramic dish that fits inside your pressure cooker. Put the first tortilla on the base. Add some of the sauce, then sprinkle with coriander (reserve some to garnish), drizzle over spoonfuls of soured cream and some of the cheese. Repeat the layers until you have used all the tortillas, then finish with soured cream and cheese. Loosely cover the top with foil.

CONTINUED . . .

TORTILLA LASAGNA
CONTINUED . . .

Wash out your pressure cooker and add 2cm (¾in) of water. Put the tin or dish on a trivet (or directly on the base if it is too deep for your cooker). Close the lid and bring up to high pressure. Adjust the heat to just high enough to maintain the pressure and cook for 10 minutes. Remove from the heat and leave to drop pressure naturally.

Remove the tin or dish from the cooker and leave to stand for a further 10 minutes if you have time. If you want to brown the cheese, you can do so by returning the tin or dish to your multicooker and using an air fryer lid, or by placing the tin or dish under a medium grill (broiler) for a few minutes.

Cut into wedges, sprinkle with the reserved coriander and, if you wish, serve with pickled jalapeños or a squeeze of lime, perhaps with some greens on the side.

A VERY QUICK
FILLING FOR TACOS

Serves 4

2 tbsp olive oil

1 red onion, cut into wedges

300g (10½oz) sprouting broccoli,
trimmed

2 avocados, peeled, stoned and diced

4 ripe tomatoes, diced

Juice of 2 limes

Sea salt and freshly ground
black pepper

TO SERVE

8 warmed corn tortillas (optional)

A few coriander (cilantro) leaves

½ tsp chilli flakes or chilli powder,
smoked if possible

I admit, I can eat a pile of this with no carb element whatsoever and have served it without tortillas as a lunch for two.

If you happen to have some cooked beans, you could add those too – black or pinto for preference. But try it without all the cheese and cream additions. There is always the temptation to add a lot to tacos but often they're better without.

Heat half the oil in your pressure cooker. When hot, add the red onion and sauté over a high heat until it has taken on a little colour, then add the sprouting broccoli. Stir to coat with the oil, then add a splash of water (50ml/1¾fl oz should be enough) and season with salt and pepper. Close the lid and bring up to high pressure. Cook for 1 minute, then immediately remove from the heat and fast release.

Put the avocados and tomatoes in a large bowl and pour over the lime juice. Season with salt. Stir through the cooked vegetables. Serve as is or use to fill warmed tortillas, garnished with the coriander and chilli.

CURRIED POUTINE

Serves 4

1 tbsp olive oil or coconut oil

A few curry leaves, if you have them

1 onion, finely chopped

200g (7oz) minced (ground) or finely diced beef

4 garlic cloves, grated (minced)

10g (¼oz) piece of ginger, grated (minced)

1 tbsp your favourite curry powder or use the basic spice mix (see page 241)

1 tsp chilli powder

2 tbsp tomato purée

2 tbsp tamarind paste (optional)

600ml (21fl oz) beef stock

1 tsp Bovril (optional)

TO SERVE

1 portion of Sautéed Potatoes (see page 196), chip-shop chips or oven chips (French fries)

200g (7oz) cheese curds, halloumi or paneer, diced and brought to room temperature

Sliced chillies (optional)

Coriander (cilantro) leaves (optional)

There is a story behind this dish. My partner, Shariq, who as you can probably tell from his name has South Asian ancestry, spent some time post-university working as a lumberjack in Canada. He returned with a love of Canadian food, especially poutine (think cheesy chips with gravy), which has become a top comfort food in our house. And while it is a moveable feast, made with leftover gravy from a roast, or the liquor from so many casseroles or curries, this fusion has become the favourite – I frequently double or triple this recipe so I can keep some in the freezer.

The original recipe, from Quebec, uses cheese curds; there's nothing like the rich, buttery curds I can get from Neal's Yard, but when I don't have them, halloumi works very well; so does paneer, if a little mild in flavour. And I don't think anyone would complain if you just melted lots and lots of Cheddar over the top.

You don't have to make the potatoes from scratch – chip-shop chips or oven chips work fine (might even be better!). Which makes this the perfect Friday night, too-tired-to-cook-properly dinner.

Heat your pressure cooker and add the oil. When hot, add the curry leaves, if using, and allow them to crackle before adding the onion and beef. Stir over a high heat until the meat is browned, then stir in the garlic, ginger, curry powder, chilli powder, tomato purée and tamarind, if using. Stir well to combine, then add the stock and Bovril, if using. Stir to make sure the base of the cooker is completely deglazed then close the lid. Bring to high pressure then adjust the heat so it is just high enough to maintain the pressure. Cook for 10 minutes, then remove from the heat and leave to drop pressure naturally.

Using a stick blender if you have one (transfer to a jug blender if not), blitz the gravy for a few seconds to thicken. The aim is a consistency that isn't completely smooth – a bit like the texture of canned oxtail soup with its little nuggets of beef.

Arrange the fried potatoes in shallow bowls and add the cheese curds. Make sure the gravy is piping hot, then ladle over the potatoes and curds. Top with chillies and coriander, if using, and serve immediately.

SON-IN-LAW
EGGS

Serves 4

2 tbsp olive oil, plus an extra 4 tbsp for the cripsy shallots (optional)

4 shallots or onions, thinly sliced into rings (optional)

8 eggs, at room temperature

1 tsp your favourite curry powder or use the basic spice mix (see page 241), optional

FOR THE SAUCE

50g (1¾oz) palm or soft light brown sugar

2 tbsp fish sauce

2 tbsp tamarind paste

1 tsp sriracha or other chilli sauce (optional)

Salt

TO SERVE

Buttered toast

Sliced chillies

A few sprigs of coriander (cilantro) or Thai basil

TIP

If your eggs aren't at room temperature, put them in a bowl of warm (not hot) tap water for a few minutes.

An excuse to show off how good pressure-cooked eggs are - but really, who doesn't love some combination of eggs on toast? In our house it is rare that spice isn't added too, so I have adulterated the classic sweet/sourness of these eggs with a touch of curry powder and hot sauce. But you can leave them out if you prefer. These eggs are also great as a carb-free snack - or as part of a main meal with rice and vegetables alongside.

If you want to make crispy shallots or onions to serve, heat 4 tablespoons of the oil in a frying pan (skillet) - use one large enough to hold all the eggs. Add the shallots and fry until crisp. Transfer to paper towel to drain the excess oil and wipe out the pan.

Pour 2cm (¾in) of water into your pressure cooker. Place a trivet and a steamer basket in the cooker and put the eggs in the basket. Close the lid and bring up to low pressure. Cook for 3½ minutes and fast release. Immediately plunge the eggs in cold water or run under a cold tap. Peel - you will find that, because they have been cooked under pressure, even though they are mollet (soft) eggs the shells and membrane will just slip off.

Put all the sauce ingredients in a saucepan with a pinch of salt and 50ml (1¾fl oz) of water. Heat through gently, stirring constantly, until the sugar has dissolved and a smooth sauce has formed. Keep warm.

Heat 2 tablespoons of oil in a large frying pan (use the same one, if you made crispy shallots). Stir in the curry powder, if using, then add the eggs. Fry, turning regularly until they start to brown and develop a crust.

Cut the eggs in half and arrange over toast or on a platter - the centres should be squidgy. Drizzle over the sauce, then garnish with crispy shallots, chillies and herbs.

HARISSA-SPICED CHICKEN LIVERS

Serves 4

1 tbsp olive oil

1 small red onion

400g (14oz) chicken livers, trimmed

1 tbsp harissa paste

1 tbsp tomato purée

2 tsp sherry vinegar

1 tbsp capers (optional)

A few parsley, mint or coriander (cilantro) leaves, finely chopped

Sea salt and freshly ground black pepper

TO SERVE

Buttered toast or warm flatbreads

A squeeze of lemon juice

A few salad leaves

We eat chicken livers at least once a fortnight in our house - even the organic ones are relatively cheap and they are really nutritious. I always seem to have jars of harissa and other chilli pastes to use up - you could use any sort here.

Heat your pressure cooker and add the oil. When hot, add the onion and chicken livers and cook over a high heat until the livers are seared all over. Stir in the harissa paste, tomato purée and some salt and pepper, then deglaze the pan with 100ml (3½fl oz) of water.

Close the lid and bring up to high pressure then adjust the heat until it just high enough to maintain the pressure. Cook for 1 minute, remove from the heat and leave for another minute before fast releasing the rest of the pressure. Stir in the vinegar and capers, if using, followed by the chopped herbs.

Spoon the chicken livers over the toast or pile into flatbreads and squeeze over the lemon juice. Serve with some salad leaves.

SPICED POTATOES WITH FLATBREADS

Serves 4

1 tbsp olive oil or ghee

1 tsp cumin seeds

A few curry leaves (optional)

1 onion, finely chopped

750g (1lb 10oz) waxy potatoes, thinly sliced

4 garlic cloves, finely chopped

1 chilli (any), finely chopped

2 tbsp finely chopped coriander (cilantro) stems, plus a few leaves to garnish

1 tsp ground turmeric

1 tbsp tamarind paste or tomato purée

150g (5½oz) kalettes (kale sprouts) or other greens

½ lemon or lime, for squeezing

Grated (shredded) cheese, such as mature Cheddar (optional)

Sea salt and freshly ground black pepper

TO SERVE (OPTIONAL)

Soft flatbreads or pittas

Mango chutney or zhoug

Sliced chillies, pickled or fresh

Sliced red onions

This is an adaptation of my mother-in-law's jeera aloo to which I have added greens. It is quite a dry dish so although I do cook it to serve with other curries, the main reason I make it is to stuff into flatbreads for lunch. If I'm doing this, I will grate over a mound of cheese and let it melt onto the potatoes and greens before piling it into the flatbread with some lime pickle, mango chutney, or similar: I can't recommend highly enough the spiced medlar chutney made by Eastgate Larder if you can get it. A little zhoug is also excellent; pickled chilli and sliced onion also works.

Heat your pressure cooker and add the oil or ghee. When hot, add the cumin and curry leaves, if using. Wait until they start to crackle then add the onion. Fry quite briskly until the onion starts to brown, then add the potatoes. Stir for a couple of minutes, then add the garlic, chilli, coriander stems and turmeric. Stir for a further couple of minutes, then season with salt and pepper.

Check the base of your pan and add a little water to deglaze it if necessary – this is especially important with this recipe because potatoes, being starchy, tend to stick to stainless steel. Add another 100ml (3½fl oz) of water, then close the lid and bring up to high pressure. Adjust the heat so it is just high enough to maintain the pressure, then cook for 3 minutes. Remove from the heat and fast release. Stir to make sure the base is still clean. Whisk the tamarind paste or tomato purée with another 100ml (3½fl oz) of water, then pour this over the potatoes. Stir briefly again then add the kalettes to the cooker. Close the lid and bring up to high pressure again. Immediately remove from the heat and fast release.

Squeeze over a little lemon or lime juice, then sprinkle with coriander. If you want to add cheese, sprinkle this over now and put the lid back on, leaving it to melt in the residual heat. Pile into flatbreads or split pittas and serve with some chutney, chillies and red onion slices, if you wish.

THE MEATBALL SANDWICH

Serves 4

FOR THE MEATBALLS

400g (14oz) minced (ground) beef, pork or lamb

50g (1¾oz) breadcrumbs

1 tsp dried oregano

1 tsp garlic powder

1 egg

50ml (1¾fl oz) double (heavy) cream

Sea salt and freshly ground black pepper

FOR THE SAUCE

2 tbsp olive oil

1 onion, finely chopped

3 garlic cloves, finely chopped

1 tsp dried oregano

400g (14oz) can tomatoes

½ tsp chilli flakes or your choice of chilli paste

1-2 sprigs of basil

100g (3½oz) Cheddar, grated (shredded)

1 ball of mozzarella, sliced

TO SERVE

1 red onion, finely sliced

1 tbsp red wine vinegar

1 long baguette

Butter for spreading (optional)

100g (3½oz) rocket (arugula)

These meatballs can also be turned into a one-pot pasta or bean dish, served over baked potatoes, or just on their own with a big pile of greens. You can make the meatballs or buy them; just use this recipe for the sauce and pressure cooking method.

To make the meatballs, mix all the ingredients together and season with plenty of salt and pepper. Divide and shape into 16 meatballs. Set aside while you make the sauce or, if you want to brown the meatballs before cooking them through, sear them briefly in the oil (I usually only bother with one side), then remove.

Heat your pressure cooker and add the oil. When hot, add the onion and garlic, and stir briefly - the onion should help deglaze the base. Add the oregano and tomatoes, swill the can with 50ml (1¾fl oz) of water and add this to the cooker too. Sprinkle in the chilli flakes or stir in the paste and season with salt and pepper. Stir well to make sure the base is completely deglazed.

Return, or add, the meatballs to the cooker and arrange the basil on top. Close the lid and bring up to high pressure. Adjust the heat so it is just high enough to maintain the pressure and cook for 10 minutes. Remove from the heat and leave to drop pressure naturally.

Fish out the basil. Sprinkle over the Cheddar and add the sliced mozzarella. Close the lid again - the cheeses will start to melt as you prepare the remaining ingredients.

While the meatballs and sauce cook, soak the red onion in the red wine vinegar. When you are ready to assemble, strain. Split the baguette lengthways, stopping just short of splitting it in two, and butter it if you like. Arrange the rocket along the crease. Spoon the meatballs, sauce and cheese over the rocket and top with the red onions. Cut into 4 pieces and serve immediately.

CHILLI CHEESE NACHOS

Serves 4

1 tbsp olive oil

1 red onion, diced

1 red (bell) pepper, diced

1 green (bell) pepper, diced

3 garlic cloves

200g (7oz) pumpkin or squash (peeled weight), diced

200g (7oz) sweetcorn

750g (1lb 10oz) cooked beans – black/red/pinto or a mixture (see page 231 for cooking instructions)

1 tbsp chipotle or ancho chilli paste

2 bay leaves

1 tbsp chilli spice mix (see page 241) or use a shop-bought version

400g (14oz) can chopped tomatoes

Sea salt and freshly ground black pepper

TO SERVE

1 bag tortilla chips, any flavour

3 tbsp pickled jalapeños, roughly chopped

200g (7oz) hard cheese, such as Cheddar or similar, grated (shredded)

250g (9oz) soured cream (optional)

1 small bunch of coriander (cilantro)

This is a super-speedy vegetarian chilli, served over cheesy chilli nachos – or, if you prefer, you can put the nachos on top of the chilli and either crisp under the grill or using an air-fryer lid, if you have that kind of multicooker. Either way, the combination of crisp and chewy as the nachos soften in the chilli is so very satisfying.

You can of course add all kinds of other things to this – I sometimes add diced chicken at the beginning of the cooking process, or make the chilli with beef (see the variation below). But it is excellent just as it is. Also try it on baked potatoes, with plenty of butter and cheese.

Heat your pressure cooker and add the oil. When hot, add the onion and peppers. Sauté for 2–3 minutes, then stir in all the remaining ingredients. Swill the tomato can with 100ml (3½fl oz) of water and add this to the cooker too. Stir to make sure the base of the cooker is completely deglazed and season with salt and pepper.

Close the lid and bring up to high pressure. Adjust the heat so it is just high enough to maintain the pressure and cook for 2 minutes. Remove from the heat and leave to drop pressure naturally.

To serve, arrange the tortilla chips over a baking tray and sprinkle with the jalapeños and cheese. Put under a hot grill (broiler) until the cheese has melted and started to brown. Divide between bowls and dollop with soured cream, if using, before ladling the chilli over the top. Garnish with plenty of chopped coriander.

VARIATION

Turn into a quick chilli con carne by adding 500g (1lb 2oz) minced (ground) beef with the onion and browning. Omit the squash and sweetcorn, reduce the weight of beans to 500g, and cook for 10 minutes instead of 2.

HOMEMADE BAKED BEANS WITH JACKET POTATOES

Serves 4

4–6 baking potatoes, each around 200g (7oz)

Butter or olive oil (optional)

150g (5½oz) grated (shredded) hard cheese, such as Cheddar (optional)

FOR THE BEANS

500g (1lb 2oz) haricot (navy) or cannellini beans, soaked overnight or quick soaked (see page 230)

1 onion

2 cloves

400ml (14fl oz) passata

2 tbsp tomato purée

1 tsp garlic powder

1 tbsp maple syrup

500ml (17fl oz) stock or water

Sea salt and freshly ground black pepper

This recipe is in this chapter despite it being all homemade, because it is amazingly quick – there is literally a minute's prep, and that can be done well in advance. You can reheat the beans and lightly brown the potatoes under the grill at the same time: dinner on the table in moments.

Why make your own baked beans? So many reasons but in part because the price of a can has gone through the roof and these are much cheaper – especially if you cook them in the same pot as the jacket potatoes – meaning that the energy cost is almost incidental. This recipe gives the equivalent of about six cans, so you have some for another day too.

This is my basic recipe – you can add bacon or sausage, sliced vegetables such as carrot and celery, chilli them up... but honestly, the simple way is probably best.

First prepare the potatoes. Pierce each one all over with a skewer, making sure you go right to the centre – this will help prevent them building up steam and splitting. Place in a steamer basket.

Put the soaked beans in your pressure cooker. Stud the onion with the cloves and add to the cooker along with all the other ingredients for the beans. Season with salt and pepper and stir.

Put a trivet in the cooker – it should come just above the height of the beans – and place the steamer basket containing the potatoes on top. Sprinkle the potatoes with salt.

Close the lid and bring up to high pressure. Adjust the heat so it is just high enough to maintain the pressure. Cook for 20 minutes, then remove from the heat and leave to drop pressure naturally.

Remove the potatoes, the basket and the trivet from the pressure cooker. If you want to crisp up the potatoes, you can put them under a low grill (broiler) for a few minutes, turning regularly. Fish out the clove-studded onion and serve the beans with the potatoes, and, if you like, butter or oil and top with cheese.

A BIT MORE
TIME ON
YOUR
HANDS...
WEEKEND
SPECIALS

Nothing takes a prohibitively long time in the pressure cooker and these recipes are no exception – they don't require what I consider to be lengthy cooking. But there are certain types of dishes I reserve for the weekend; for me, a pot-roast chicken or a proper taco feast (despite the concept of Taco Tuesday), are not midweek meals. It isn't just about the finished dish – although some of these do feel like occasion meals and I'm glad of that – it's the process. I don't want to be marinating or soaking during the week when I rarely plan what we're going to eat from day to day. I'm certainly not going to consider making stuffings, fillings or pastry – perhaps not even tortillas (making them in my house is a Saturday afternoon family affair and, yes, of course we buy them ready-made too). But these are all lovely things to do when I have a bit more time to potter.

BACON AND EGG KIMCHI RAMEN

Serves 4

1 tbsp olive oil

8 rashers (strips) smoked back bacon

10g (¼oz) piece of ginger, cut into matchsticks

3 garlic cloves, sliced

1 small bunch of coriander (cilantro), stems and leaves separated and chopped

1.8 litres (63fl oz) stock (chicken, vegetable, dashi, even ham)

2 tbsp dark soy sauce

250g (9oz) kimchi (including juice)

4 nests of dried medium egg noodles

200g (7oz) sprouting broccoli, kai lan (Chinese broccoli), green beans, spinach or wedges of Chinese leaf (Napa cabbage)

TO SERVE

4 spring onions (scallions), finely chopped

2-4 mollet (medium-boiled) eggs (see page 126)

Sesame seeds

Sesame or chilli oil

A full meal soup, this, and one that is much loved in our house. It's the comforting combination of smoky/savoury bacon, heat and noodles (thank you, David Chang). It is very quick to make and assemble once you have cooked the eggs, but I do like to leave the broth to infuse for a little while, which is why I don't consider it an instant meal. Having said that, it is a really good prepare-ahead dish as so many of the elements can be cooked and reheated – the eggs, bacon, broth, even the noodles.

This method does reduce the amount of broth you end up with because the noodles are cooked in it. If you like a lot of broth, cook the noodles in the pressure cooker separately – just cover in freshly boiled water, then follow the same instructions.

Heat your pressure cooker and add the oil. When hot, add the bacon and fry on both sides until it starts to render out fat and brown. Remove from the cooker and set aside. Add the ginger, garlic and finely chopped coriander stems. Sauté for 1 minute, then pour in your stock and the soy sauce.

Close the lid and bring up to pressure. Immediately remove from the heat and leave to drop pressure naturally. Leave to stand off the heat for 30 minutes if you have the time.

Strain the kimchi from its juice and add the juice to the cooker. Push the noodles into the broth making sure they are submerged. Pile your choice of green vegetables on top. Close the lid and bring up to high pressure again, then immediately remove from the heat and fast release. Stir to break up the noodles. Drop the bacon rashers into the broth just to heat through.

Divide the noodles, vegetables and bacon between bowls. Add chopped kimchi to the bowls and ladle over the broth. Garnish with the chopped coriander leaves, spring onions, eggs and sesame seeds. Drizzle over sesame or chilli oil before serving, or offer at the table.

POT-ROAST CHICKEN

Serves 4

1.4–1.8kg (3lb 2oz–4lb) whole chicken

1 tbsp olive oil

A few whole garlic cloves, pierced

1 sprig of tarragon

15g (½oz) butter

100ml (3½fl oz) red or white wine

200g (7oz) puréed tomatoes
(fresh or canned)

A few garlic cloves

Large sprigs of thyme and tarragon

2 bay leaves

350g (12oz) can olives (150g/
5½oz drained weight), pitted;
or I like anchovy-stuffed here

2 tbsp capers

Zest of 1 lemon

Sea salt and freshly ground
black pepper

Your choice of greens, such as the
Quick-Steamed Greens on page 195,
or salad, to serve (optional)

This has a Mediterranean vibe to it, with flavours of an Italian cacciatore – perfect for a relaxed summer's lunch. It will probably give you more sauce than you need, but any leftovers make an excellent pasta sauce or the base for a quick soup.

I rarely want to eat this with anything more than a floppy green salad or lightly steamed greens, but in winter, I might add a dauphinoise, too.

Consider this first step optional but preferable. The day before you want to cook the bird, remove all packaging, place on a plate and sprinkle with a fine layer of salt. Cover with paper towel and leave in the fridge overnight.

At least an hour before you want to start cooking, remove the chicken from the fridge to bring it up to room temperature.

Heat your pressure cooker and add the oil. When hot, put the garlic cloves and tarragon in the cavity of the chicken. Sear the chicken all over until well browned. This does require a bit of manoeuvring so you can do this in a frying pan (skillet) if you prefer, then transfer it to the cooker.

Smear the chicken breasts with butter and sprinkle with black pepper.

Put the wine, tomatoes, garlic cloves and herbs in the cooker. Close the lid and bring up to high pressure. Adjust the heat so it is just high enough to maintain the pressure and cook for 15 minutes. Remove from the heat and leave to drop pressure naturally.

Transfer the chicken to a serving platter, making sure any liquid inside the cavity is poured back into the cooker. At this stage you can crisp up the skin again if you like, by putting it under a hot grill (broiler), or using an air-fryer lid or a blowtorch.

Stir the olives, capers and lemon zest into the sauce. Leave to stand off the heat for a few minutes – it will thicken up a little in that time.

Serve with greens or a simply dressed salad.

BEEF BRISKET TACOS WITH BROTH AND BLACK BEANS

Serves 4

1 tbsp oil, plus extra for frying the tortillas

1 onion, halved

1 head of garlic, cloves separated and peeled

1kg (2lb 4oz) rolled brisket or similar, preferably in one piece

1 tbsp taco spice mix or the Mexican-style spice mix on page 241

2 tbsp chilli paste (any sort)

2 tbsp tomato purée

3 bay leaves

100ml (3½fl oz) strong black coffee (optional)

1.5 litres (52fl oz) chicken or beef stock or water

1 tbsp red wine vinegar

Sea salt and freshly ground black pepper

OPTIONAL EXTRA

250g (9oz) black beans, unsoaked

TO SERVE

Corn tortillas

Plus any extras you like, including:

Avocado, sliced and tossed in lime juice and salt

Red onion, sliced and tossed in lime juice and salt

Sprigs of coriander (cilantro)

IF YOU MUST

Soured cream

Grated (shredded) cheese

Right now, if I were to ask either of my children what they would like for dinner, I would bet my life on at least one of them saying tacos. They love the ritual of it, all the colour of the accoutrements they can add at table - and, when we have time at the weekend (and I have the patience), they love making the tortillas too.

This recipe is based on a birria, a Mexican stew that was traditionally made with goat or lamb, so you could use either. But beef has become a popular version and it is my preference here. I make a lot of broth with this recipe - it sits in the fridge and freezer, ready to come out whenever I need a pick-me-up. I might add a judicious glug of rum or similar too - it makes for an interesting bullshot.

For ease, I've used a chilli paste. However, most supermarkets stock a good range of chillies and they are also easy to source online if you want to use fresh ones instead of a paste. I suggest using a combination of 4 ancho, 2 guajillo and 1 chipotle. Simply deseed and toast in a dry frying pan, then add at the same time as the bay leaves.

The beans - well, they cook beautifully alongside the beef and the little starch they release helps the texture of the broth, so it is well worth including them.

Heat your pressure cooker and add the oil. When hot, add the onion, cut side down. Fry until it has built up some colour, then add the garlic and toss around for a minute. Remove from the cooker. Season your meat with salt and pepper, and sear on all sides. Remove from the cooker and stir in the spice mix, chilli paste, tomato purée, bay leaves and coffee. Stir to make sure the base is completely deglazed, then return the meat, onion and garlic to the cooker. Pour over the stock and red wine vinegar and season with salt and pepper. If you are cooking the beans at the same time, add them too.

Close the lid and bring up to high pressure. Reduce the heat so it is just high enough to maintain the pressure and cook for 1 hour. Remove from the heat and leave to drop pressure naturally.

Take the meat from the cooker and use a couple of forks to break it into chunks (see tip), discarding any big pieces of fat as you go. Strain the broth into a saucepan or heatproof jug and remove the bay, onions and garlic cloves from the beans. The garlic cloves can be mashed into the broth. Reserve the black beans for another meal (see note).

You can serve the meat as is, moistened with a little broth, or fry in oil to crisp it up around the edges, before moistening with some of the broth.

To serve the tortillas in a traditional way, heat 1 tablespoon of oil in a frying pan (skillet). Dip each tortilla in the broth so they are lightly coated in the oil which will have collected on top. Fry briefly on both sides. Repeat with the remaining tortillas, adding more oil to the frying pan as necessary. Ladle the broth into individual cups for both dipping and drinking. Serve the meat with the tortillas and as many extras as you like.

NOTE

The cook time is long for the beans, but the tomato purée, salt, etc, mean they keep their integrity wonderfully while being perfectly creamy within. And the best thing is that they don't unduly flavour the broth, just thicken it very slightly. The beans will keep for up to a week in the refrigerator – use them to make the Rice and Peas (page 209) or the Korean-inspired Ginger Vegetables (page 90).

TIP

You don't have to shred all the meat for tacos; you can leave some or all of it in a whole piece. It will firm up as it cools and is very good sliced, cold or hot, in sandwiches. My son was very happy when I broke up a couple of thick slices, warmed them through with a little broth, then stirred through loads of grated (shredded) cheese to put in a sloppy Joe!

STEAK AND MUSHROOM SUET PUDDING

Serves 4

2-3 tbsp beef dripping or olive oil

400g (14oz) beef or venison (either chuck or braising), diced

2 tbsp plain (all-purpose) flour

1 onion, sliced

2 celery sticks, sliced

1 carrot, halved lengthways and sliced

50g (1¾oz) smoked bacon lardons (optional)

200g (7oz) mushrooms, sliced if large

3 garlic cloves, finely sliced

100ml (3½fl oz) red wine

100ml (3½fl oz) well-flavoured beef stock

1 tbsp Dijon mustard

A bouquet garni or a bay leaf, a sprig of thyme, a sprig of parsley

65g/2¼oz (drained weight) canned smoked mussels or oysters finely chopped (optional)

Sea salt and freshly ground black pepper

FOR THE PASTRY

200g (7oz) plain (all-purpose) flour, plus extra for dusting

1 tsp baking powder

1 tsp dried thyme

25g (1oz) butter, chilled and diced, plus extra for greasing

75g (2¾oz) suet (shredded lard)

A suet pudding is an excellent Sunday lunch alternative to a roast, and while it is a bit more involved than bunging a large joint of meat into the oven, it is easy in that both elements can be prepared ahead. Suet puddings used to be filled out with oysters and mussels, as they were so cheap and readily available; I include smoked ones because I really love the smoky, umami flavour they add to the gravy. Beef is traditional but I sometimes use venison – actually, you can use any casserole meat you like. I have been known to use leftover lamb curry, putting turmeric and mustard in the suet crust, and serving with the Spiced Potatoes on page 128.

First make the filling. Heat your pressure cooker and add 1 tablespoon of dripping or oil. Dust the meat with flour and season with salt and pepper. Sear on all sides, making sure a decent crust develops. Don't crowd the base of the pan – add the meat in two batches if necessary.

Remove the meat to a plate and add another tablespoon of dripping or oil. Add the onion, celery, carrot and bacon, if using, and sauté over a high heat until starting to colour. Add the mushrooms and continue to cook until browned, then stir in the garlic.

Pour in the wine and stir to make sure the base of the cooker is completely deglazed. Add the stock and mustard, then return the meat, plus any juices, to the cooker. Season with more pepper and add the bouquet garni. Close the lid and bring up to high pressure. Adjust the heat so it is just high enough to maintain the pressure. Cook for 15 minutes, then leave to drop pressure naturally. Strain off and reserve the liquor and stir in the mussels or oysters, if using.

While the beef is cooking, make the pastry. Put the flour and baking powder in a bowl and add a generous pinch of salt and the dried thyme. Rub in the butter, then stir in the suet. Add just enough water, a tablespoon at a time, to make a firm, fairly dry dough – it needs to hold together but not be so sticky you can't roll it out. Cut off a quarter of the dough for the lid. Flour a work surface and roll out the rest to a circle about 30-35cm (12-14in).

Grease a 1-litre (35fl oz) pudding basin (ovenproof bowl) then line with the pastry, letting it overhang the edges. Pile the strained meat and vegetables into the lined basin, removing the bouquet garni. Ladle over a little of the cooking liquor. Roll the remaining pastry into a round large enough to top the basin. Place over the beef, then fold over the overhanging pastry and press to completely seal.

Fold a pleat in a piece of foil or baking paper and use to cover the basin. Secure with string or a rubber band.

Pour 2cm (¾cm) of freshly boiled water into your pressure cooker. Add a trivet or a folded cloth and place the pudding on top. Loosely cover the cooker with the lid, then return the water to the boil. When you can see steam starting to appear, steam for 15 minutes (this gives the raising agent a chance to work), tightly close the lid and bring up to high pressure. Adjust the heat so it is just high enough to maintain the pressure and cook for 45 minutes. Remove from the heat and leave to drop pressure naturally.

Remove the pudding and leave to stand for 5 minutes, then remove the foil or paper and run a palette knife around its rim. Turn out onto a plate. Reheat the reserved cooking liquor and serve as a gravy alongside the pudding.

CHICKPEA AND ROAST CAULIFLOWER CHAAT

Serves 4

FOR THE CHICKPEAS

1 tbsp coconut oil

3 garlic cloves, finely chopped

500g (1lb 2oz) dried chickpeas (garbanzo beans), rinsed

1 tbsp tamarind paste

1 tsp garam masala or curry powder

FOR THE CAULIFLOWER

1 tbsp coconut oil

A few curry leaves (optional)

1 tsp nigella or cumin seeds

1 medium cauliflower, cut into small florets

1 tsp garam masala or curry powder

Sea salt and freshly ground black pepper

TO GARNISH/SERVE

2 shallots or 1 red onion, finely sliced

Juice of 1 lime or ½ lemon

200g (7oz) yogurt

2 tbsp mango chutney or similar

100g (3½oz) baby spinach leaves

100-125g (3½-4½oz) sev or similar (Bombay mix will work at a pinch)

Seeds of a small pomegranate

2 medium chillies, finely chopped

Leaves from a small bunch of coriander (cilantro), chopped

1 tsp amchoor (optional)

Despite the very long list of ingredients, this is amazingly quick to assemble, with a delicious combination of sweet, sour, spice. It is also flexible: no chickpeas? Use red kidney beans or sliced new potatoes. No spinach? Salad leaves will be just as good. No cauliflower? Any vegetable amenable to this kind of instant roast will work.

Sev is a thin crispy-fried noodle, the sort you get in Bombay mix. It comes in different flavours with varying degrees of spice.

First prepare your garnishes. Sprinkle the shallots or onion with ½ teaspoon of salt, pour over the lime or lemon juice and leave to marinate. Mix together the yogurt and chutney in a bowl and season with salt and pepper. Set aside.

To cook the chickpeas, heat your pressure cooker and add the coconut oil. Once melted, add the garlic and sauté for a couple of minutes. Add the chickpeas, tamarind paste and garam masala or curry powder and 150ml (5½fl oz) of water. Season. Give a quick stir, then close the lid, bring up to high pressure and immediately remove from the heat. Leave to drop pressure for 2 minutes, then release the rest of the pressure. Transfer the contents to a bowl to start cooling.

Wash out your cooker and reheat it. When it is hot, add the coconut oil. Once melted, add the curry leaves and seeds. Once they start to crackle add the cauliflower and sauté over a high heat for 2 minutes until it starts to colour. Stir in the garam masala and 75ml (2¼fl oz) of water. This will create a lot of steam - quickly click the lid into place and bring up to high pressure. Remove from the heat immediately and leave to drop pressure for 30 seconds before releasing the rest of the pressure.

To assemble, arrange the chickpeas over a large platter adding just a little of the cooking liquor, then stir through the spinach. Sprinkle over some of the sev, then top with the cauliflower. Give everything a stir, then sprinkle over more sev. Drizzle over a couple of spoonfuls of the chickpea cooking liquor. Drain the shallots and sprinkle them over the platter, along with the pomegranate seeds, chillies and plenty of coriander. Top with more sev and sprinkle amchoor over the lot. Serve the spiced yogurt on the side.

PORK AND SAUSAGE HOTPOT

Serves 4

2 tbsp olive oil

8 large pork sausages (I like Lincolnshire, always)

500g (1lb 2oz) belly pork, diced

150g (5½oz) smoked bacon lardons

150ml (5fl oz) red wine

3 tbsp tomato purée

2 tbsp Dijon mustard

2 tsp light soft brown sugar

1–2 tbsp treacle

500g (1lb 2oz) haricot (navy) beans, soaked overnight in salted water or quick soaked (see page 230)

2 carrots, thickly sliced

3 bay leaves

1 large sprig of thyme

4 garlic cloves

1 onion, peeled but left whole

4 cloves

Stock or water

Sea salt and freshly ground black pepper

If I had to choose one dish that takes me back to my childhood, it would be this hotpot. It's a kind of cross between Boston baked beans and cassoulet, the sort of thing my mum would make by the vat for a Bonfire Night party, or on a snow day. The associations are strong: wood smoke, snow drifts, fun...

This is slightly more involved than many of the recipes in this book, but it is worth making from scratch, not least because it is much cheaper to buy dried beans than forking out for the four or five cans you would need to get the equivalent cooked amount.

Heat your pressure cooker and add 1 tbsp of the oil. When hot, lightly brown the sausages on all sides, then remove. Add the remaining oil and sear the belly pork too, until well browned and starting to render out some fat. Remove from the cooker and fry the bacon lardons until coloured.

Pour in the wine and stir vigorously to completely deglaze the base of your cooker. Stir in the tomato purée, mustard, sugar and 1 tablespoon of the treacle.

Drain the soaked beans and add to the cooker along with the carrots, herbs and garlic. Stud the onion with the cloves and push into the beans. Stir in the pork belly and put the sausages on top.

Add just enough stock or water to cover the beans and season with salt and pepper.

Close the lid and bring up to high pressure. Adjust the heat so it is just high enough to maintain the pressure and cook for 20 minutes. Remove from the heat and leave to drop pressure naturally.

Taste and adjust the seasoning as you like – you may want to add more mustard, sugar or treacle. Fish out the onion and remove the cloves – you can break up the onion and return it to the pot if you like.

Serve in bowls, or ladled over baked potatoes and/or sprinkled with cheese.

POACHED CHICKEN
WITH RICE

Serves 4

1 whole chicken (any size), untrussed or the equivalent in pieces

1 head of garlic, cloves separated but unpeeled

30g (1oz) piece of ginger, thinly sliced

Sea salt

FOR THE RICE

2 tbsp oil or chicken fat skimmed from the cooking liquor

2 garlic cloves, crushed or grated (minced)

300g (10½oz) jasmine rice, well rinsed

FOR THE SAUCE

3 tbsp soy sauce

3 tbsp rice wine

1 tsp honey

A few drops of toasted sesame oil

10g (¼oz) piece of ginger, grated (minced)

TO GARNISH

½ cucumber, sliced or smashed

A bunch of spring onions (scallions), shredded

Hot sauce or chilli oil

This is based on Hainanese chicken, one of the blandest looking of dishes, but absolutely packed with flavour. The instructions below are for a whole chicken, but you can make this with a couple of legs, drumsticks or even breasts (preferably on the bone, for flavour) if you prefer a smaller portion. The same timings will work, as long as you make sure the chicken is covered with cold water when you start.

The method here is based on the concept of 'zero-minute chicken' and can be used for any poached chicken dish you fancy.

Rub the whole chicken or pieces with 1 teaspoon of salt, then put in your pressure cooker with the garlic and ginger. Cover with cold water (or light chicken stock, if you have some) and bring up to high pressure. Remove from the heat immediately and leave to drop pressure naturally. Prepare a bowl of iced water, large enough to drop the chicken into – this halts the cooking and improves the texture of the meat. Leave in the iced water for 15 minutes, then remove, drain thoroughly and pat dry on paper towel. Strain the poaching liquor into a jug or bowl. Squeeze the garlic cloves from their skins into the liquor. Wipe out the cooker, ready to cook the rice.

Heat your pressure cooker and add the oil or chicken fat. When hot, add the garlic. Sauté for a minute, then add the rice and stir until well coated. Add 450ml (16fl oz) of the poaching liquid and season with salt. Bring to high pressure, then adjust the heat until it is just high enough to maintain the pressure. Cook for 3 minutes. Remove from the heat and leave to drop pressure naturally.

While the rice cooks, make the sauce by mixing all the ingredients together. Set aside.

Slice the chicken or pull off in chunks (on or off the bone) and serve with the rice, cucumber, spring onions and some hot sauce or oil. You can also turn this dish into a broth if you prefer – simply reheat the rest of the cooking liquor and pour over.

ROAST LAMB WITH RED WINE AND ROSEMARY GRAVY

Serves 4

Half a leg of lamb, thick end

A few sprigs of rosemary

1 head of garlic, broken into cloves

2 tbsp olive oil or dripping

1 onion, thickly sliced

150ml (5½fl oz) red wine

250ml (9fl oz) stock – chicken, lamb or vegetable

Sea salt and freshly ground black pepper

OPTIONAL EXTRAS

300g (10½oz) carrots, cut into chunks

500g (1lb 2oz) potatoes, cut in chunks if large

This doesn't really take any time at all, but you do have to take care with the searing and it does feel as if a roast belongs in a weekend chapter. I resisted roasting lamb in the pressure cooker for years, sticking with either beef for a fast roast, or lamb shoulder for a slow one. The main reason for this is that a boneless leg of lamb is quite expensive and I wasn't sure how a bone-in joint would fare with the fast cook time. I shouldn't have worried: it works brilliantly and there is the added bonus of softened marrow melting into the gravy.

You can cook vegetables alongside the lamb if you like – the method does allow for this. But I would rather keep the lamb warm, make the Dauphinoise on page 204, cook some greens (Brussels sprout tops for preference) and perhaps some roast carrots and parsnips (see page 197) too. A whole roast dinner, done in the pressure cooker, in no time at all.

An hour before you want to start cooking, remove the lamb from the fridge to bring it up to room temperature. Make a note of the weight, as this affects the cooking time. As soon as you take it out of the fridge, cut slits all over the flesh and stuff with some of the rosemary. Peel and thinly slice one of the garlic cloves and stuff those into the slits too. Sprinkle both cut sides of the lamb with salt and leave for 1 hour.

When you are ready to start cooking, heat your pressure cooker and add the oil or dripping. When hot, sear the lamb on all sides, making sure a dark, rich crust develops. Don't skimp on this, as it makes such a difference to the finished dish. A good indication of when the lamb is ready to be turned is if it will lift off the base of your cooker without too much reluctance.

CONTINUED . . .

ROAST LAMB WITH RED WINE AND ROSEMARY GRAVY CONTINUED . . .

Transfer the lamb to a plate. Add the onion to the cooker and sauté for a couple of minutes, then pour in the red wine. Stir to make sure the base is thoroughly deglazed, then add the stock, all but one of the remaining garlic cloves and most of the rest of the rosemary. Season with salt and pepper.

Put a trivet in your pressure cooker and add the steamer basket. Put the lamb in the basket and put the carrots and potatoes, if simultaneously cooking, around the lamb. Pour any lamb juices from the plate into the cooker.

Close the lid and bring the pressure cooker up to pressure. Adjust the heat so it is just high enough to maintain the pressure. For a 500g (1lb 2oz) piece of lamb, cook for 5 minutes for rare, 6 minutes for medium rare and 7 minutes for medium. Add an extra minute for every additional 500g (1lb 2oz). Remove from the heat and leave to drop pressure naturally.

Remove the lamb (and vegetables), from the cooker and loosely cover with foil to rest for at least 10 minutes (at this point you can cook your vegetables separately if you prefer). Strain the cooking liquor, pushing through the garlic flesh and onion to thicken into a gravy. Reheat before serving with the lamb.

WHOLE STUFFED SQUASH

Serves 4

1 squash or pumpkin, around 1.5kg
(3lb 5oz)

1 garlic clove, halved

FOR THE FILLING

1 tbsp olive oil

50g (1¾oz) bacon, finely chopped
(optional)

15g (½oz) butter

1 leek, trimmed and cut into rounds

A splash of white wine or cider (or use
water)

1 tsp dried sage or mixed herbs

1 garlic clove, crushed or grated
(minced)

1 sweet, crisp apple, peeled, cored
and diced

15g (½oz) pecans, chopped (optional)

1 tbsp maple syrup

1 tsp mustard powder

100g (3½oz) stale sourdough
bread, diced

50ml (1¾fl oz) single (light) cream

125g (4½oz) grated (shredded) hard
cheese, such as Gruyère or Cheddar

Sea salt and freshly ground
black pepper

I've done autumn in a bowl (Mushroom and Jerusalem Artichoke Soup, page 22) and this is autumn on a plate. It is the kind of relaxed cooking I will do after a walk to the farmers' market on a Saturday. The dish is surprisingly economical, cobbled together from a few bits and pieces.

I have found that for a 6-litre (1½ gallon) pressure cooker, a 1.5kg (3lb 5oz) squash is probably around as large as you can go: do check before you start – but you can use the filling to stuff smaller, individual squashes if you prefer. The cook time is dependent on the thickness of the pumpkin flesh, rather than the overall weight and it is best to use one that isn't too firm. Onion (red kuri), acorn or kabocha squash is perfect. And don't forget, you can eat the skin as well as the flesh.

First prepare the squash. If necessary, trim the base slightly so it will stand upright. Cut into the top at a 45-degree angle, working all the way around until the top comes off cleanly. Scoop out all the seeds and stringy bits around them. Rub the flesh with the garlic halves.

To make the filling, heat your pressure cooker and add the oil. When hot, add the bacon, if using, and cook until crisp and brown. Transfer to a large bowl and add the butter to the cooker. Once melted, add the leek and stir to coat. Add a splash of wine, cider or water, stir to deglaze the base and close the lid. Bring up to high pressure and immediately fast release.

Add the leek to the bowl with the bacon, along with the herbs, garlic, apple, pecans (if using), maple syrup, mustard and bread. Stir in the cream and 75g (2¾oz) of the cheese, season with salt and pepper and stir thoroughly. Pile the filling into the pumpkin, pressing down if necessary. Top with the remaining cheese.

CONTINUED . . .

WHOLE STUFFED
SQUASH CONTINUED . . .

Put a trivet in your cooker and top with a steamer basket. Line the
steamer basket with a foil sling for easier removal of the pumpkin post
cooking. Place the pumpkin inside. Tuck the pumpkin cap down the
side of the pumpkin.

Close the lid and bring up to high pressure. Adjust the heat so it is
just high enough to maintain the pressure and cook for 15 minutes.
Remove from the heat and leave to drop pressure naturally. Check
that the centre of the filling is piping hot – if it isn't (this does
sometimes happen if you are using a particularly thick-fleshed
pumpkin), return to high pressure for a further 5 minutes.

Using the sling, carefully transfer the pumpkin from the cooker to
a serving plate or bowl. Serve in thick slices with any loose crumbs
of the stuffing spooned over.

TIP

The filling is based on a savoury bread pudding and is a really
good way to use up stale bread. If you want to bake it on its own,
add a beaten egg with the cream, pile it into a heatproof dish,
cover with baking paper and sit on a trivet or folded cloth.
Cook as above for 15 minutes.

LAMB BIRYANI

Serves 4

1kg (2lb 4oz) stewing lamb, cut into large chunks (a mix of leg and trimmed shoulder is ideal)

1 tbsp olive oil or ghee

1 tsp mustard seeds

4 green cardamom pods

½ cinnamon stick

2 cloves

2 bay leaves

½ tsp coriander seeds

1 tsp garam masala

1 small bunch of coriander (cilantro), chopped

2 green chillies, finely sliced

1 tbsp tomato purée

300ml (10½fl oz) chicken or vegetable stock or water

500g (1lb 2oz) basmati rice, well rinsed

15g (½oz) butter

A large pinch of saffron (optional)

Sea salt and freshly ground black pepper

FOR THE MARINADE

150g (5½oz) yogurt

15g (½oz) piece of ginger, grated (minced)

4 garlic cloves, crushed

Zest and juice of 1 lime

A pinch of ground turmeric

½ tsp ground cardamom

¼ tsp cayenne

This recipe isn't particularly labour-intensive, but I do marinate the meat, as I like to use a leaner cut. Also, there are several stages, which you do need to take your time over. I like to serve it with roast carrots (see page 197), and there would be uproar in my house if I didn't serve at least a dal (see the simple one on page 81) and flatbreads alongside.

First marinate the lamb. Put the ingredients for the marinade in a large bowl and add 1 teaspoon of salt and plenty of black pepper. Stir together then add the lamb. Mix to combine, then cover and leave in the fridge for at least a couple of hours, but preferably overnight.

When you are ready to cook, prepare the fried onions – these are mainly a garnish, but some are stirred through the rice. Heat your pressure cooker or a large frying pan (skillet). Add the oil or ghee and, when hot, fry the onions over a medium heat until crisp and brown. Season with salt and pepper and stir in the cumin. Drain on paper towel.

To cook the lamb, heat your pressure cooker and add the oil or ghee. When hot, add first the whole spices then the marinated lamb, scraping off any excess yogurt (although it should be quite dry). Stir until the lamb has started to colour, then stir in the garam masala, coriander, chillies and tomato purée. Add the stock or water and season with salt and pepper. Stir to make sure the base is completely deglazed.

Close the lid and bring up to high pressure. Adjust the heat to maintain the pressure and cook for 15 minutes. Remove from the heat and leave to drop pressure naturally.

FOR THE FRIED ONIONS

2 tbsp vegetable oil or ghee

3 onions, thinly sliced into crescents

1 tsp ground cumin

TO FINISH

Coriander (cilantro) sprigs

Sliced green chillies

Lime wedges

Open the lid and remove the meat, straining the liquid into a measuring jug. Check the base of the cooker is clean and return the meat to the cooker. Stir half the fried onions into the rice. Sprinkle the rice mixture over the meat. If necessary, top up the reserved cooking liquor with water to give 750ml (26fl oz). Pour this over the rice – make sure that all the rice is submerged. Season with salt and pepper.

Melt the butter in a small pan or microwave. Add the saffron, swirl it around a bit, then pour in a trail over the rice.

Close the lid and bring up to high pressure. Adjust the heat so it is just high enough to maintain the pressure and cook for 3 minutes only, then remove from the heat and leave to drop pressure naturally. Remove the lid. Fold a tea towel or cloth in half, place over the cooker and rest the lid on top. Leave, off the heat, to steam for at least 10 minutes – this will really make a difference to the texture of your rice.

When you are ready to serve, transfer the biryani to a large serving platter, stirring so the lamb is mixed through. Garnish with the remaining fried onions, coriander sprigs, sliced chillies and lime wedges.

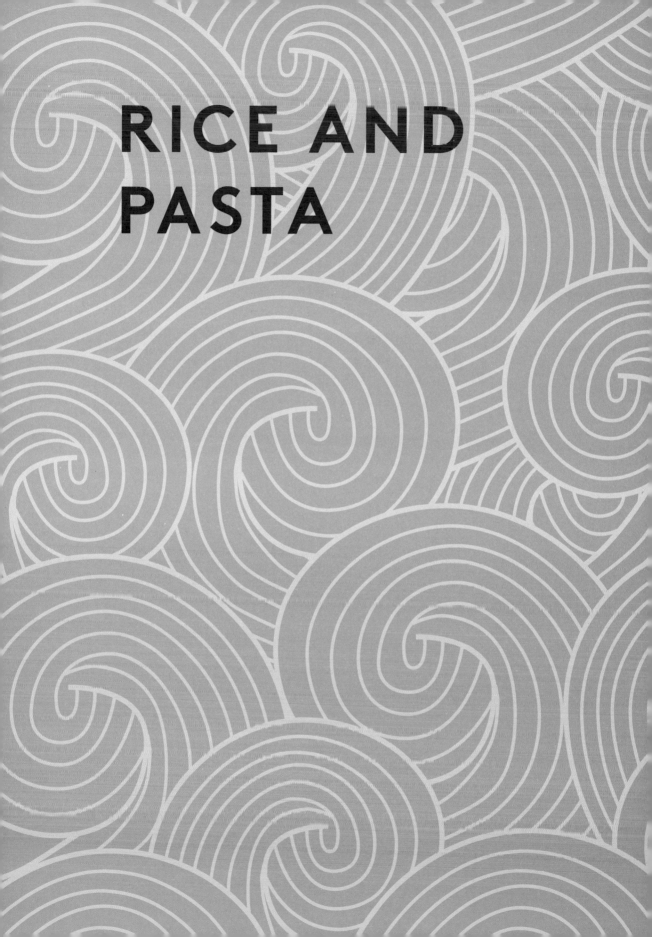

RICE AND PASTA

These are the type of meals that are mainstays in most people's homes – quick pasta and rice dishes are often the default when navigating a busy week. Pressure cooking reduces the stress further by speeding up the process as well as combining the cooking, as frequently one pot is used for both sauce and carb elements. This is the absorption method, where the sauce and the added stock/water combine to provide just enough liquid to cook the grain. What this means in practical terms is that the whole dish can be ready in the time it can take to bring a large pot of water for pasta to the boil.

A quick word on pasta. You can also cook pasta without sauce, if you already have a batch of sauce made up or are just wanting to stir in something raw like pesto. To do so, heat a couple of tablespoons of olive oil in your pressure cooker, add the pasta and season with salt and pepper. Cover with water (or stock if you prefer). Bring up to high pressure and cook for 4 minutes – it will usually take less time than a pasta using the absorption method. You can also cook it for 1 minute, remove from the heat and leave it to drop pressure for 5 minutes. If you are making a sauce which needs pasta cooking liquid (which will have starch in it), add a bit more water than usual.

Please use all of these recipes as blueprints. If you work within their parameters, you can adapt them infinitely to suit your own tastes and use up whatever you have at hand.

SPICY PASTA

Serves 4

2 tbsp olive oil

1 onion, finely chopped

3 heaped tbsp 'nduja

1 tsp dried thyme (optional)

A pinch of fennel seeds

500g (1lb 2oz) short pasta

200g (7oz) cherry tomatoes

50ml (1¾fl oz) vodka (optional)

75ml (2¼fl oz) single (light) cream

Sea salt and freshly ground
black pepper

TO SERVE

Parmesan, grated

A few basil leaves

Chilli flakes

This pasta uses 'nduja, a soft, spreadable, sausage from Calabria, which adds a good savoury heat and needs very little else. To make it vegetarian I would use a Calabrian chilli paste, harissa or chipotle in smaller quantities (2 teaspoons to start with, more at the end if necessary).

The vodka is optional but does help mellow and sweeten the sauce somehow, just as it does with a plain tomato sauce.

Heat your pressure cooker and add the oil. When hot, add the onion and sauté for 2–3 minutes, then add 2 tablespoons of the 'nduja. Cook over a gentle heat, breaking it up constantly with the back of a wooden spoon. Add the thyme, if using, and fennel seeds, and add the pasta. Stir, then add just enough water to cover. Season with salt and pepper. Drop the cherry tomatoes on top.

Close the lid and bring up to high pressure. Adjust the heat so it is just high enough to maintain the pressure, then cook for 5 minutes. Remove from the heat and fast release. Give the contents a good stir – the cherry tomatoes will burst and combine with the 'nduja. Add the vodka, if using, simmer for a couple of minutes, then taste. Add some or all of the remaining 'nduja if you want to ramp up the heat, then stir in the cream.

Leave to stand, off the heat, for another couple of minutes, then serve with plenty of Parmesan, some basil and chilli flakes for extra heat.

MUSHROOM AND MISO PASTA

Serves 4

40g (1½oz) butter

500g (1lb 2oz) mushrooms (any sort), thickly sliced

3 garlic cloves, very finely chopped

1 tbsp tamari or dark soy sauce

1 tsp rice or sherry vinegar

1 onion, very finely chopped

100g (3½oz) destemmed kale or chard leaves, roughly torn

400g (14oz) short pasta

2 tbsp miso paste (any sort)

75ml (2¼fl oz) single (light) cream

Parmesan or similar, finely grated, to serve

Sea salt and freshly ground black pepper

When friends and readers know I am working on a new cookery book, they frequently make suggestions or come up with conventional recipes they have tried that they aren't quite sure how to convert to pressure cooking. This is one such dish. I was initially unsure about the miso but it works really well.

Heat your pressure cooker and add 15g (½oz) of the butter. As soon as it melts and foams, add the mushrooms and fry briskly until they are well browned. Add one of the chopped garlic cloves, stir for 1 minute then pour over the tamari and vinegar. Remove the contents from the cooker.

Melt another 10g (¼oz) of butter in the cooker and add the onion and the rest of the garlic. Stir for 1 minute, then stir in the kale or chard, followed by the pasta. Season with salt and pepper. Mix 1½ tbsp of the miso with enough water to make a pourable consistency, pour this over the pasta, then add enough water to just cover the pasta. Stir to make sure the base of the cooker is completely deglazed.

Close the lid and bring up to high pressure. Adjust the heat so it is just high enough to maintain the pressure and cook for 5 minutes. Fast release. Stir the mushrooms into the pasta along with the remaining butter and the cream. Taste and add the remaining miso if you think it needs it.

Ladle into bowls with plenty of Parmesan or similar to serve.

PRESSURE COOKER RISOTTO

Still the most divisive of all pressure cooker dishes, but not among those who have already tried it – one thing I hear frequently is that this risotto method is much more achievable and stress free than the traditional way. I thought long and hard about which risotto to include here; I have written so many, but the ones I make at home are never the same twice. So I've gone with a couple of favourites: one light, the other robust and meaty. But I hope that if you follow the rice-to-liquid ratios and the timings, you can adapt all your own favourites, rather than follow mine. The cook time here is not exact as it will depend on your pressure cooker and the type of rice (carnaroli takes slightly longer than arborio).

When cooking risotto for the first time in the pressure cooker, cook for 5 minutes if using arborio, or 6 if using carnaroli. If your risotto isn't quite cooked, don't risk putting it back under pressure – the amount of starch already released into the liquid will mean it may burn before you get it up to pressure. Just leave it on a low heat, stirring occasionally, until it has cooked and make a note for next time that you will need to cook it for longer.

A LIGHT, CITRUSSY RISOTTO

Serves 4

A bunch of asparagus

2 tbsp olive oil

30g (1oz) butter

2 leeks, trimmed and finely sliced

3 garlic cloves, finely chopped

2 small courgettes (zucchini), finely sliced or grated (shredded)

Zest of 1 lemon and a squeeze of the juice (optional)

Leaves from a sprig of thyme

Leaves from a sprig of tarragon, finely chopped

300g (10½oz) risotto rice (arborio or carnaroli)

100ml (3½fl oz) white wine or vermouth

750ml (26fl oz) chicken or vegetable stock

25g (1oz) Parmesan, grated, plus extra to serve

100g (3½oz) fresh peas (optional)

Sea salt and freshly ground black pepper

This is a fresh, green risotto - perfect for late spring and summer - which also works as a very good base for other ingredients. For instance, if I am feeling extravagant, I toss white crabmeat in a little lemon juice and grated nutmeg and stir that through at the end.

Snap off the woody ends of the asparagus stalks (save for the soup on page 14). Cut off the tips - the top 5-6cm (2-2½in) - and finely chop the rest into rounds.

Heat your pressure cooker and add half the oil. When hot, add the asparagus tips. Season with salt and let them roll around in the oil for a minute, then add a splash of water. Close the lid and bring up to high pressure. Fast release immediately. Set aside the asparagus.

Remove any liquid from the cooker. Add the remaining oil and half the butter. When the butter has melted, add the leeks, asparagus stems, garlic and courgettes. Cook for a couple of minutes, then add the lemon zest and herbs. Add the rice and stir until the grains are glossy with butter.

Pour in the wine and bring to the boil. When it has almost evaporated, pour in the stock and season with salt and pepper. Close the lid and bring up to high pressure. Adjust the heat so it is just high enough to maintain the pressure and cook for 5-7 minutes, then fast release. Check the rice: if it isn't quite cooked, leave over a low heat for a couple more minutes.

Stir in the remaining butter and the Parmesan and beat until the risotto is creamy. The courgettes will break up, but that is the aim. Stir in the peas, If using, and either stir in the asparagus or treat as a garnish. Put the lid on for a few moments, just to reheat the asparagus.

Serve with extra Parmesan at the table and perhaps a squeeze of lemon.

A ROBUST,
HEARTY RISOTTO

Serves 4

1 tbsp olive oil

30g (1oz) butter

250g (9oz) sausages, skinned

1 onion, finely chopped

1 tsp dried sage

150g (5½oz) squash, diced (optional)

300g (10½oz) risotto rice (arborio or carnaroli)

25g (1oz) sunblush tomatoes (smoked if possible), puréed

100g (3½oz) tomatoes, preferably fresh, puréed

100ml (3½fl oz) red or white wine

750ml (26fl oz) chicken or vegetable stock

25g (1oz) Parmesan, grated

Sea salt and freshly ground black pepper

TO SERVE

10g (¼oz) butter

A few fresh sage leaves

Grated Parmesan

This is the family favourite throughout the winter months. You can of course use any type of sausages – we favour very garlicky ones like a Toulouse, or the British equivalent, Rutland, or an Italian one, which is often also flavoured with fennel.

Heat your pressure cooker and add the oil and half the butter. When hot, add the sausages and onion. Stir to break up the meat and brown it thoroughly. Stir in the sage and squash, if using, followed by the rice. When the rice is glossy, stir in the puréed tomatoes, followed by the wine. Bring to the boil and stir to deglaze as wine evaporates.

Pour in the stock and season with salt and pepper. Close the lid and bring up to high pressure. Adjust the heat so it is just high enough to maintain the pressure and cook for 5–7 minutes, then remove from the heat and fast release.

Beat in the remaining butter and the Parmesan until creamy.

Melt the 10g (¼oz) butter in a separate frying pan (skillet). When it foams, add the sage leaves and fry until crisp.

Serve the risotto with extra Parmesan and the sage leaves, drizzling over the butter to finish.

MEATY MACARONI CHEESE

Serves 4

1 tbsp olive oil

1 onion, finely chopped (see tip)

1 carrot, grated (shredded)

1 celery stick, finely diced

500g (1lb 2oz) minced (ground) beef or sausagemeat

3 garlic cloves, finely chopped

1 tsp garlic powder

1 tsp ground oregano

100ml (3½fl oz) red or white wine

50g (1¾oz) tomato purée

500g (1lb 2oz) macaroni (or any other type of short pasta)

1 litre (35fl oz) chicken or beef stock

200ml (7fl oz) milk or a mixture of milk and single (light) cream

200g (7oz) Cheddar or similar hard cheese, finely grated (shredded)

Sea salt and freshly ground black pepper

This is a cross between a bolognese and a mac 'n' cheese: creamy, rich, savoury and very comforting. You can use any type of ground meat you like, but I usually go for beef or sausagemeat. And if you want to keep it as a quick bolognese without all the cheese, that will work too.

Heat your pressure cooker and add the oil. When hot, add the onion, carrot and celery and sauté for a few minutes until starting to colour. Add the meat and brown thoroughly, then stir in the garlic, garlic powder and oregano.

Pour in the wine, followed by the tomato purée. Stir until well mixed then add the macaroni. Stir again and pour over the stock, making sure the base of the cooker is completely deglazed. Season with salt and pepper.

Close the lid and bring up to high pressure. Adjust the heat so it is just high enough to maintain the pressure, cook for 5 minutes then remove from the heat. Release the pressure manually, but in a controlled way just in case the steam becomes starchy.

Stir in half the milk, followed by 150g (5½oz) of the cheese. Stir until the cheese has melted into the sauce, then finish with the remaining milk and cream. Serve immediately with the rest of the cheese sprinkled over.

TIP

If you have some soffritto (page 236) at hand, use 4 tablespoons in place of the onion, carrot and celery here. Simply start the recipe by heating the oil and browning the meat, then add the soffritto at the same time as the garlic.

CHICKEN, TOMATO AND PEPPER RICE

Serves 4

2 roast red (bell) peppers (see page 100)

100g (3½oz) fresh or canned tomatoes

1 Scotch bonnet, deseeded

2 tbsp olive or coconut oil

1 large red onion, finely diced

600g (1lb 5oz) chicken meat (I prefer thigh), diced

4 garlic cloves, finely chopped

2 bay leaves

1 large sprig of thyme

1 tbsp your favourite curry powder or use the basic spice mix (see page 241)

2 tbsp tomato purée

300g (10½oz) basmati rice, well rinsed

25g (1oz) butter

450ml (16fl oz) chicken or vegetable stock or water

Sea salt and freshly ground black pepper

TO SERVE

A few sprigs of flat-leaf parsley or coriander (cilantro), finely chopped

Lemon or lime wedges

Hot sauce (optional)

My inspiration for this comes from jollof rice; I hope it captures some of the exuberance and depth of the flavour of the original West African dish.

I will happily eat this as soon as the pressure has dropped but there is no denying that leaving it to steam very gently afterwards will help the texture enormously. So if you have time, I recommend it.

Put the peppers, tomatoes and Scotch bonnet in a food processor and blitz until smooth. Set aside.

Heat your pressure cooker and add the oil. When hot, add the onion and chicken and sauté until the chicken has lightly coloured on the outside. Add the garlic, herbs, curry powder, tomato purée and the blitzed pepper mix. Stir until it has a rich aroma and has reduced a little – you don't want it looking too wet.

Stir in the rice and butter, and season with plenty of salt and pepper. Pour in the stock or water and stir to make sure the base of the cooker is completely deglazed. Close the lid and bring up to high pressure. Adjust the heat so it is just high enough to maintain the pressure and cook for 3 minutes. Remove from the heat and leave to drop pressure naturally.

The rice is now perfectly good to eat, but if you want to create a bit of a crust on the base (it will give it a slightly smokier flavour), you can cover the cooker with a tea towel or cloth, place the lid loosely on top and leave over a very low heat for around 10 minutes. This will help fluff up the grains and lightly brown the rice.

Serve with chopped parsley or coriander and lemon or lime wedges for squeezing over. And some people might want a drop or two of hot sauce too.

ONE-POT STEAMED FISH WITH RICE

Serves 4

4 fillets of salmon or white fish (all of a similar thickness)

2 garlic cloves, crushed

5g (⅛ oz) piece of ginger, grated (minced)

Zest and juice of ½ orange

50ml (1¾fl oz) dark soy sauce or tamari

1 tsp gochujang or ½ tsp chilli powder

1 tsp toasted sesame oil, plus extra for greasing and to serve

200g (7oz) sprouting broccoli, halved lengthways

1 carrot, cut into ribbons

300g (10½oz) basmati or jasmine rice, well rinsed

Sea salt and freshly ground black pepper

TO SERVE

4 spring onions (scallions), sliced into rounds

Sesame seeds

Chilli oil or more toasted sesame oil

A classic rice bowl, this, which is usually dependent on leftover rice, or on everything being cooked separately before being assembled. However, with the pressure cooker, you can cook everything together at the same time. One pot instead of three is not bad going.

First prepare the fish. Season the fillets with salt and pepper and put in a bowl. Mix together the garlic, ginger, orange zest and juice, soy sauce and gochujang, then pour over the fish.

Take a piece of foil, large enough to make a parcel of the fish and vegetables, and grease with a little toasted sesame oil. Place the fish on the foil and pour over any remaining marinade. Top with the broccoli, followed by the carrot ribbons. Seal the parcel.

Put the rice in the base of your pressure cooker with the toasted sesame oil. Season with salt and pour in 450ml (16fl oz) of water. Place the trivet in the cooker and balance the foil parcel on top (or, if it is easier, you can tuck the parcel on top of a steamer basket instead).

Close the lid and bring your cooker up to high pressure. Adjust the heat so it is just high enough to maintain the pressure, and cook for 3 minutes. Remove from the heat and leave to drop pressure naturally. Open the lid, remove the foil parcel and put a tea towel or cloth over the top of the cooker. Replace the lid, loosely, and continue to steam, off the heat, for 5 minutes.

To assemble, divide the rice, fish and vegetables between bowls. Top with the spring onions and sesame seeds and drizzle over any of the remaining sauce. Serve with more sesame or chilli oil.

ONE-POT GNOCCHI

Serves 2

2 tbsp olive oil

50g (1¾oz) bacon lardons (optional)

1 small onion, very finely chopped

1 courgette (zucchini), diced

3 garlic cloves, finely chopped

100ml (3½fl oz) white wine

250g (9oz) gnocchi

100g (3½oz) baby spinach

75g (2¼oz) Dolcelatte, crumbled

Sea salt and freshly ground
black pepper

A few chilli flakes, to serve (optional)

This uses ready-prepared gnocchi, either vacuum-packed or fresh from the chill counter, both of which are readily available. It works well as an almost-instant dinner with maybe a salad on the side.

Gnocchi takes no time at all to cook conventionally, but you still have to boil water first before you cook it. The method here saves water as well as time and fuel. I have, however, made this a two-portion dish because the gnocchi really needs to be in a single layer in your pressure cooker if it is going to cook properly.

Heat your pressure cooker and add the oil. When hot, add the bacon, if using, and onion and sauté over a medium-high heat until lightly browned. Stir in the courgette (zucchini) and the garlic and cook for a couple of minutes. Pour in the wine and stir to deglaze the base of the cooker thoroughly. Add the gnocchi, lightly shaking the cooker so they spread evenly in a single layer. Season with salt and pepper, then arrange the spinach on top.

Close the lid and bring up to high pressure. Immediately remove from the heat and leave for 30 seconds before fast releasing the pressure. Put back over a low heat as you stir in the cheese – it will form a creamy sauce around the gnocchi.

Serve immediately, with a few chilli flakes if you want a little heat.

LAMB AND PEA PASTA

Serves 4

1 tbsp olive or coconut oil

1 onion, finely chopped

10g (¼oz) piece of ginger, grated (minced)

3 garlic cloves, crushed or grated (minced)

300g (10½oz) minced (ground) lamb

1 small bunch of coriander (cilantro), stems and leaves separated and finely chopped

1 tbsp curry powder or use the basic spice mix (see page 241)

25g (1oz) red lentils, unrinsed

250g (9oz) peas or petits pois (defrosted if frozen)

100g (3½oz) tomatoes, fresh or canned, puréed

250g (9oz) short pasta

Stock or water

Sea salt and freshly ground black pepper

TO SERVE

150g (5½oz) Cheddar or similar hard cheese, grated (shredded)

2 green chillies, sliced

Every pressure cooker book I write has a version of keema peas – the South Asian classic of spiced mince and petits pois – which has been a staple in my house forever. Then, last year, my son started pestering me to put it in a pasta bake and wow, was it good. So here it is – yet another fusion dish that my family loves.

Heat your pressure cooker and add the oil. When hot, add the onion, ginger, garlic and lamb and stir until the meat has lightly browned. Stir in the coriander stems (reserve the leaves), curry powder, red lentils, peas, tomatoes and pasta. Season with plenty of salt and pepper and stir to combine, making sure that the base of the cooker is completely deglazed.

Add just enough stock or water to cover the pasta, then close the lid. Bring up to high pressure and adjust the heat so it is just high enough to maintain the pressure. Cook for 5 minutes and fast release. Stir well.

Now, options – you can simply sprinkle with the cheese, chopped coriander leaves and sliced chillies and leave on a low heat, covered, so the cheese melts. Alternatively, you can brown the cheese either by first wrapping the handle in foil then placing your pressure cooker under a grill (broiler) or by using an air-fryer lid. Or you can transfer the lot to an ovenproof dish, sprinkle with cheese, coriander and chillies, and brown under the grill. Whichever you choose, I can guarantee it will be good.

HOT LUNCHES, ON THE GO

This chapter came about when I started sharing how easy it is to make really fast lunches first thing in the morning with a pressure cooker and a few basic ingredients – often including leftovers and batch-cooked ingredients. For years I had been making them for my children as a healthier option to school lunches or a box of sandwiches and snacks. These recipes aren't just applicable to children, though – I know from the response to my Thermos stories on Instagram that many people use the ideas for their work lunches. By using up leftovers and small amounts of vegetables, it works out far cheaper than endless rounds of sandwiches.

There are a few rules I follow, which are specific to how food behaves when it is kept hot. I avoid overwhelmingly strong cheeses or anything fishy – these are not good after several hours. Parmesan and condiments like kimchi are best kept separately and added later.

Carb-based meals are cheaper – I rotate pasta, various rices and grains, beans, chickpeas, noodles and potatoes.

The food must be piping hot when it is ladled into a Thermos flask; this does impact on what I cook. Anything too wet or brothy will take too long to cool down to be practical to eat during a limited lunchbreak. If the time factor isn't an issue, most of the soups in the first chapter should work well too.

Many other recipes in this book will work well in a Thermos – any of the curries, casseroles, stews, chunkier soups with some kind of carbohydrate. The grain recipes here are limited to rice, but quinoa and bulgar wheat are even quicker to cook. In the mornings, I will only bother with grains that take longer to cook like brown rice, spelt, barley and freekeh if I have some already cooked in the fridge or frozen.

Let me give you an example of how it might work. The curried chickpeas recipe (page 187) has 50g (1¾oz) basmati rice. Everything else in that particular dish will cook perfectly well made with quinoa or bulgar wheat instead (1 minute high pressure as opposed to 3). Or, if you have some cooked brown rice, add 125g (4½oz) of that in place of the 50g (1¾oz) raw basmati and reduce the cook time to 1 minute, natural release.

There are a few things which will help you make this type of lunch. First of all, my 'freezer essentials' always include frozen vegetables such as peas, broad beans, spinach (leaf and chopped) and sweetcorn.

I batch-cook beans and chickpeas and, unless they are in a sauce, I open-freeze them (ie freeze them on a tray so they don't stick together) before transferring to containers. I also chop up and freeze coriander stems to use by the tablespoon, and I try to have tomato sauce, soffritto, and the onion, garlic and ginger paste ready too.

Sometimes I defrost meals alongside cooking the carb element. As an example, if I have frozen a 2-portion curry and want to add it to rice, I will put the rice and water necessary for cooking it in the cooker, put the frozen block of curry on top, cook for 3 minutes and natural release as usual. The curry will have defrosted and be piping hot (unnervingly it remains a block until you stir it in) and the rice will be cooked.

This is all about giving yourself options and being flexible.

The dishes in this section are all 2 portions. I figure that most people might be happy eating the same thing twice but not four times (although of course, you can tweak it each day).

CHIPOTLE BEANS AND RICE

Fills 2 x 500ml (17fl oz) Thermos flasks

1 tbsp olive oil

½ red onion, finely diced

½ red or green (bell) pepper, diced

50g (1¾oz) squash (optional) diced

50g (1¾oz) bacon, sausage or any leftover meat (optional)

1 tbsp tomato purée

1–2 tsp chipotle paste, or similar

1 tsp dried oregano

2 tbsp finely chopped coriander (cilantro) stems

½ tsp garlic powder or 1 clove garlic, finely chopped

1 tsp ground cumin

250g (9oz) beans – black, pinto or red kidney

100g (1½oz) sweetcorn (frozen is best)

50g (1¾oz) basmati rice, well rinsed

Sea salt and freshly ground black pepper

TO SERVE

Lime wedges

Grated (shredded) cheese

Tortillas or nachos

This is great as a Thermos lunch, but it also makes a really good all-in-one filling for a couple of burritos. However, I would only recommend doing this if eating right away, or if the burritos can be chilled down and reheated properly.

Heat your pressure cooker and add the oil. When hot, add the onion, pepper, squash and meat, if using, and stir for a couple of minutes. Add the tomato purée, hot paste then the herbs, garlic and cumin. Finally add the beans, sweetcorn, rice and 100ml (3½fl oz) of water. Stir to make sure the base is completely deglazed. Season with salt and pepper.

Close the lid and bring up to high pressure. Adjust the heat so it is just high enough to maintain the pressure and cook for 3 minutes. Remove from the heat and leave to drop pressure naturally. Stir to make sure everything is evenly distributed and spoon into hot Thermos flasks.

Include wedges of lime, a pot of grated cheese and perhaps a couple of tortillas or a few nachos in the packed lunch.

SAUSAGE AND BEANS

Fills 2 x 500ml (17fl oz) Thermos flasks

1 tbsp olive oil

1 small onion, sliced

4 sausages, broken up or sliced

½ red (bell) pepper, diced

1 courgette (zucchini), diced

2 kale or cavolo nero leaves, shredded

100g (3½oz) squash, diced (optional)

250g (9oz) cooked beans or chickpeas (garbanzo beans)

100g (3½oz) peas or sweetcorn kernels, fresh or frozen

1 tbsp tomato purée

1 tsp dried oregano

A pinch of chilli flakes

Sea salt and freshly ground black pepper

This is a comforting one. I keep all kinds of sausages in the freezer – smoked, merguez, fresh, all wrapped in 1-2 portions so I can get them out the night before for ready to cook in the morning. You can also use leftover meatballs or mince or fry some bacon.

Heat your pressure cooker and add the oil. When hot, add the onion and sausages. Sear on all sides, then add the red pepper, courgette, kale, squash (if using), beans and the peas or sweetcorn. Cook for a couple of minutes, then stir in the tomato purée, and pour in around 100ml (3½fl oz) of water. Stir to make sure the base of the cooker is completely deglazed, then season with salt and pepper and sprinkle in the oregano and chilli flakes.

Close the lid and bring up to high pressure. Immediately remove from the heat and leave to drop pressure naturally. Spoon into hot Thermos flasks.

LEFTOVER CHICKEN RISOTTO

Fills 2 x 500ml (17fl oz) Thermos flasks

1 tbsp olive oil

25g (1oz) butter

1 small onion, finely chopped

2 garlic cloves, finely chopped

½ tsp dried herbs (any)

100g (3½oz) cooked chicken, ham or sausage, chopped

150g (5½oz) risotto rice

50ml (1¾fl oz) white wine (optional)

375ml (13fl oz) stock (preferably chicken, made from the carcass, see page 234)

100g (3½oz) frozen peas or sweetcorn, or 4 cubes frozen spinach

Sea salt and freshly ground black pepper

15g (½oz) Parmesan, grated (shredded), to serve

I call this leftover chicken risotto as it is one of the Thermos meals I make after a roast chicken dinner. But you could use fresh chicken too if you prefer – it will easily cook in the time needed for the rice – just add it with the onion.

A Thermos risotto will take any leftovers really – a bit of chopped ham, some sliced sausage (chorizo is popular) as well as frozen vegetables. My children like frozen sweetcorn in theirs; I find it a bit sweet, even with ham, but peas, broad beans or spinach all work brilliantly.

Beat in some butter and put the Parmesan in a little pot for sprinkling. I add a few chilli flakes too.

Heat your pressure cooker and add the oil and half the butter. When the butter starts to foam, stir in the onion, garlic, herbs, meat and rice. Stir until the rice is glossy with oil and butter, then add the wine, if using. Pour in the stock and stir to make sure the base is completely deglazed. Season with salt and pepper. Sprinkle over the frozen vegetables.

Close the lid and bring up to high pressure. Adjust the heat so it is just high enough to maintain the pressure, cook for 5–6 minutes, then fast release. Beat in the remaining butter and ladle into hot Thermos flasks. Put the Parmesan in separate pots, for sprinkling when ready to serve.

FRIED RICE

Fills 2 x 500ml (17fl oz) Thermos flasks

1 tbsp olive oil

50g (1¾oz) cooked meat, leftover roast, bacon or Chinese sausage (all optional)

200g (7oz) vegetables – any of the following:

   1 small carrot, cut into batons

   ½ red (bell) pepper, cut into strips

   A few baby corn, cut into chunks

   ½ courgette (zucchini), cut into chunks

   A few mushrooms, sliced or halved if large

   A wedge of cabbage, shredded

   2 spring onions (scallions), cut into rounds

2 garlic cloves, finely chopped

5g (⅛oz) piece of ginger, grated (minced) (optional)

A generous pinch Chinese 5-spice

1 tbsp finely chopped coriander (cilantro) stems

150g (5½oz) basmati rice, well rinsed

100g (3½oz) frozen peas or sweetcorn

Sea salt and freshly ground black pepper

TO FINISH

2 tbsp dark soy sauce

A few drops toasted sesame oil

This will take any small amounts of vegetables you have lying around, as well as cooked or smoked meats - anything you like. I supplement the fresh with food from the freezer.

Heat your pressure cooker and add the oil. When hot, add the meat, if using, and your selection of vegetables. Sauté for 1 minute. Add the garlic, ginger, if using, 5-spice and coriander stems. Stir in the rice, frozen peas or sweetcorn. Pour in 225ml (7¾fl oz) of water and stir to make sure the base of the cooker is completely deglazed. Season with salt and pepper.

Close the lid and bring up to high pressure. Adjust the heat so it is just high enough to maintain the pressure and cook for 3 minutes. Remove from the heat and leave to drop pressure naturally. Stir in the soy sauce and toasted sesame oil, then ladle into hot Thermos flasks.

CHILLI
NOODLES

Fills 2 x 500ml (17fl oz) Thermos flasks

1 tbsp olive oil

50g (1¾oz) leftover cooked meat or minced (ground beef) (optional, only if you need to use some up)

200g (7oz) selection of vegetables, such as:

   ½ red (bell) pepper, cut into strips

   1 small carrot, julienned

   2 spring onions (scallions), chopped

   50g (1¾oz) green beans, halved

   a few baby corn, halved lengthways

   a wedge of green or Savoy cabbage, shredded

2 tbsp finely chopped coriander (cilantro) stems

5g (¼oz) piece of ginger, cut into matchsticks

3 garlic cloves, thinly sliced

1 tsp hot sauce (sriracha is ideal)

½ tsp ground turmeric

2 nests/blocks medium egg noodles

Sea salt and freshly ground black pepper

TO FINISH

2 tbsp soy sauce

A drizzle of toasted sesame oil

This is a very basic recipe for noodles and I do add all kinds of things to it. For example, I make it a bit sweet/sour by chopping up a few cubes of pineapple. It is good to use kimchi, in place of or in addition to the hot sauce. Putting the kimchi in a small pot to be added at lunchtime is better for its nutritional quality – and it will smell better that way.

Heat your pressure cooker and add the oil. When hot, add any leftover meat and the vegetables and stir-fry for a couple of minutes. Stir in the coriander stems, ginger, garlic, hot sauce and turmeric, then push everything to one side. Lie the noodles flat on the base of your pressure cooker. If you are using deep nests rather than shallow blocks, break them in half to make 4 shallower nests. Add enough water to almost cover the noodles and season with salt and pepper.

Close the lid and bring up to high pressure. Immediately remove from the heat and leave to stand for 1 minute. Release the remaining pressure. Stir in the soy sauce and toasted sesame oil, then pile into hot Thermos flasks.

FAVOURITE PACKED-LUNCH PASTA

Fills 2 x 500ml (17fl oz) Thermos flasks

2 tbsp olive oil

½ onion, finely diced (or 2 cubes of Soffritto – see page 236)

2 rashers (strips) of bacon or a chunk of chorizo or 2 sausages, all finely chopped (optional)

1 small courgette (zucchini), diced, or 4 kale leaves, shredded (optional)

½ tsp dried oregano

2 garlic cloves

2 tbsp tomato purée

20g (¾oz) red lentils, unrinsed

250g (9oz) short pasta

50g (1¾oz) cream cheese

Sea salt and freshly ground black pepper

Parmesan, grated, to serve

This is my fall-back pasta recipe for the Thermos lunch. It is economical, being based on leftovers, and I won't do certain things, like open a whole can of tomatoes or a packet of mince. Instead, it is very much a case of scouting around in the fridge and freezer. This is the favourite. Actually, anything with a smoked meat/cheese combination is always a winner.

Heat your pressure cooker and add the oil. When hot, add the onion, meat and courgette (if using) and stir until the meat has browned. Add the oregano and garlic and cook for 1 minute. Stir in the tomato purée.

Sprinkle in the red lentils and pasta. Add enough water to just cover the pasta and stir well to make sure the base of the cooker is completely deglazed. Season with salt and pepper.

Close the lid, bring up to high pressure and adjust the heat so it is just high enough to maintain the pressure. Cook for 5 minutes, then carefully fast release.

Stir in the cream cheese and leave to stand for a couple of minutes before ladling into hot Thermos flasks. Put the Parmesan in separate pots, for sprinkling when ready to serve.

CURRIED CHICKPEAS AND RICE

Fills 2 x 500ml (17fl oz) Thermos flasks

1 tbsp coconut or olive oil

1 onion, chopped

½ red (bell) pepper, diced

1 carrot, finely sliced

5g (¼oz) piece of ginger, grated (minced)

3 garlic cloves, grated (minced)

2 tbsp chopped coriander (cilantro) stems

2 tsp curry powder or use the basic spice mix (see page 241)

250g (9oz) cooked chickpeas (garbanzo beans) – see page 231 for cooking instructions

50g (1¾oz) basmati rice, rinsed

1 tbsp tomato purée

4 cubes of frozen spinach

Sea salt and freshly ground black pepper

If you have any Onion, Garlic and Ginger Paste (see page 240) ready, you can use this instead of the fresh ingredients – it will save a couple of minutes' chopping time.

Heat your pressure cooker and add the oil. When hot, add the onion, red pepper, carrot, ginger, garlic and coriander. Cook for a minute or two, then stir in the curry powder, chickpeas and rice. Add 100ml (3½fl oz) of water and stir in the tomato purée. Stir to make sure the base of your cooker is completely deglazed, and season with salt and pepper. Drop the cubes of spinach on top.

Close the lid and bring up to high pressure. Adjust the heat so it is just high enough to maintain the pressure and cook for 3 minutes at high pressure, then remove from the heat and leave to drop pressure naturally.

Give a quick stir to make sure the spinach is evenly dispersed, then spoon into hot Thermos flasks.

PASTA WITH CHICKPEAS, HALLOUMI AND HARISSA

Fills 2 x 500ml (17fl oz) Thermos flasks

1 tbsp olive oil

1 small onion, finely diced

½ courgette (zucchini), diced

2 large cavolo nero leaves, shredded

100g (3½oz) cooked chickpeas (garbanzo beans) or beans

½ x 200g (7oz) block of halloumi, diced

1 tbsp smoked harissa (or any chilli paste)

25g (1oz) red lentils, unrinsed

200g (7oz) short pasta

Lemon juice

Sea salt and freshly ground black pepper

This one came about when the kids both wanted the comfort of pasta and cheese because they'd both got colds. I was planning on 'nduja, but had none left, so I came up with this instead. The halloumi wasn't left over (who ever has a half block sitting around? Not me). But the rest, fried, was the basis of a great lunch for me and my husband.

Halloumi is a good cheese in a Thermos lunch - the flavour is creamy and very savoury without being too strong or pungent, and its bouncy, squidgy texture adds interest.

Heat your pressure cooker and add the oil. When hot, add the onion and courgette. Sauté for a couple of minutes, then add the cavolo nero, chickpeas, halloumi and harissa. Stir to combine, then sprinkle in the red lentils, followed by the pasta. Season with salt and pepper, and add just enough water to cover the pasta.

Close the lid and bring up to high pressure. Adjust the heat so it is just high enough to maintain the pressure, then cook for 5 minutes. Remove from the heat and fast release. Give the pasta a stir and add a squeeze of lemon juice.

Spoon into hot Thermos flasks.

MEAT AND
TWO VEG

Fills 2 x 500ml (17fl oz) Thermos flasks

2 tbsp olive oil

1 small onion, finely chopped
or sliced

100g (3½oz) any leftover cooked
meat or 50g (1¾oz) uncooked bacon/
sausage/chorizo

200g (7oz) unpeeled potatoes,
diced or thickly sliced

1 carrot, sliced (optional)

200g (7oz) frozen broad (fava) beans,
peas or sweetcorn

1 tsp dried herbs, depending on
your meat

4 kale or chard leaves, shredded

100ml (3½fl oz) stock or leftover
gravy

Sea salt and freshly ground
black pepper

I'm being a bit tongue in cheek here, but this is really what this meal is. All the fresh ingredients – meat, potatoes, other veg – can be substituted for any leftovers. For example, if you've got a batch of cooked potatoes in the fridge, you can use those instead and reduce the pressure-cooking time to 1 minute.

The flavours are infinitely adjustable in this. I will add dried mint or fresh rosemary for lamb, thyme for beef, sage for pork, and any of the above or tarragon for chicken. These are the traditional combinations but do as you please. If you have dried mixed herbs that don't smell of dust, they will work too.

Heat your pressure cooker and add the oil. When hot, add the onion and meat. Sauté for a couple of minutes, then add the potatoes and carrot, if using. Stir for another couple of minutes, then add your frozen vegetables, dried herbs and kale. Stir to combine, then add the stock or leftover gravy. Stir to make sure the base of the cooker is completely deglazed, then season with salt and pepper.

Bring up to high pressure and adjust the heat so it is just high enough to maintain the pressure. Remove from the heat and leave to drop pressure naturally, then divide between hot Thermos flasks.

TERYAKI CHICKEN AND MUSHROOM NOODLES

Fills 2 x 500ml (17fl oz) Thermos flasks

1 tbsp olive oil

150g (5½oz) chicken meat (any), cut into strips (optional)

100g (3½oz) mushrooms, halved if large

5g (¼oz) piece of ginger, cut into matchsticks

3 garlic cloves, thinly sliced

100g (3½oz) sprouting broccoli, roughly chopped

2 nests/blocks medium egg noodles

Sea salt and freshly ground black pepper

FOR THE TERIYAKI SAUCE

2 tbsp dark soy sauce

1 tbsp mirin

1 tsp rice wine vinegar

1 tsp light soft brown sugar OR kecap manis

1 tsp hot sauce (sriracha is good here)

TO FINISH

2 spring onions (scallions), thinly sliced

A few coriander (cilantro) leaves (optional)

A drizzle of toasted sesame oil

This will work just as well as a vegetarian meal if you don't have chicken. The chicken can be raw - it will cook in the time - or cooked.

First, whisk together the sauce ingredients.

Heat your pressure cooker and add the oil. When hot, add the chicken, if using, and stir-fry for a minute or two until lightly coloured. Add the mushrooms and cook for another minute, then add the ginger and garlic. Stir-fry for a final minute, then stir in the broccoli.

Push everything to one side and add the noodles so they can lie flat on the base of your cooker. If you are using deep nests rather than shallow blocks, break them in half to make 4 shallower nests. Add enough water to almost cover the noodles and season with salt and pepper.

Close the lid and bring up to high pressure. Immediately remove from the heat and leave to stand for 1 minute. Release the remaining pressure. Pour in the sauce and stir to combine – this will also help break up the noodles. Garnish with the spring onions, coriander and toasted sesame oil and pile into hot Thermos flasks.

A FEW
USEFUL
SIDES

At the beginning of this book I talk about using pressure cookers every day and I think it is right to say, considering side dishes, that many cooker owners forget exactly what they have at their disposal. Whether you are doing the main part of your meal in a pressure cooker or roasting, grilling, frying, etc conventionally, you will save a lot more time, fuel and water if you use your pressure cooker for your sides as well.

From talking to people about this, I realize there is a tendency to go on autopilot when it comes to cooking sides like greens. The kettle goes on, water is poured into a pan, water boils... already that is a lot of fuel and water even before you drop in the vegetables, then you have to add on the steaming/boiling time too. Compare that with the almost instantaneous method described here: unbelievably fast and the results are amazing – fresh, green, al dente. Plus – because the cook time is so fast – the nutrient preservation is much better.

In many of my recipes, vegetables are integral to the dish, or cook simultaneously in a steamer basket. But the way most people cook is to have greens or other veg on the side. I hope, once you start using the methods here, that they will become second nature. Just think how much you will save over time if you cook sides this way on a daily basis. It all adds up!

QUICK-STEAMED GREENS

This works with virtually all greens – you just have to adjust the cook time to suit your pressure cooker as they all vary very slightly.

Simply cover the base of the cooker with water – no more than 100ml (3½fl oz) – and set over a high heat. When you see some steam starting to form, add washed greens and season with salt and pepper. Close the lid and bring up to high pressure then immediately remove from the heat. For most greens, you can fast release at this point and they will be perfectly cooked – bright green and al dente. Others might take longer so leave to drop pressure naturally for 1–2 minutes.

I find that zero minutes to 30 seconds is usually enough for shredded cabbage, chard, kale, kalettes, spring greens, pak choi, kai lan, sprout tops, green beans, runner beans, broad (fava) beans, peas, cime di rapa, okra, asparagus, sliced courgettes (zucchini), leeks, sprouting broccoli, cauliflower or broccoli florets. Whole or halved Brussels sprouts, halved Little Gems or wedges of cabbage need a little longer for their centres to be knife-tender.

YOU CAN ADAPT THIS METHOD BY

- Sautéing/searing in olive oil or butter first, with added garlic or herbs, citrus zest, chilli or bacon lardons.

- Straining the greens, returning them to the cooker and simmering for another couple of minutes with cream or crème fraîche.

QUICK-STEAMED POTATOES AND ROOT VEG

Follow the method above, using the following cook times.

Potatoes and sweet potatoes, whole: 10–25 minutes (skewer all over)
Steamed new/salad potatoes, whole: 5–10 minutes depending on size
Other root vegetables, cut into chunks: 5 minutes

SAUTÉED
POTATOES

Serves 6-8

2 tbsp olive oil

1kg (2lb 4oz) small potatoes

This works best with small skin-on potatoes.

Heat your pressure cooker and add the oil. When hot, add the
potatoes. Leave to brown on one side without touching, then flip
over and brown again. Add any seasoning you like – salt, any herbs,
lemon zest, a little garlic – then pour over around 50ml (1¾fl oz)
of water and click the lid into place immediately as a lot of steam will
be created. Bring up to high pressure. Adjust the heat so it is just
high enough to maintain the pressure, cook for 3 minutes, then fast
release. Serve immediately.

HONEY-ROAST
CARROTS AND PARSNIPS

Serves 4-6

2 tbsp olive oil

750g (1lb 10oz) carrots and parsnips, peeled (optional), halved or quartered lengthways, depending on size

15g (½oz) butter

2 tsp honey

Sesame seeds

Sea salt and freshly ground black pepper

You can do either/or here, but I like cooking them together.

Heat your pressure cooker and add half the oil. When hot, add half the carrots and parsnips, cut side down, and sauté until they have taken on some decent colour on the cut sides. Remove, add the remaining oil and carrots and parsnips and sauté.

Return the first batch to the cooker and season with salt and pepper. Melt in the butter, then drizzle over the honey. If the base of the cooker needs deglazing, add around 50ml (1¾fl oz) of water and stir. After you have deglazed, if a lot of steam is still apparent, put the lid on or, if it has subsided, add another 50ml (1¾fl oz) of water. Close the lid and bring up to high pressure. Adjust the heat so it is just high enough to maintain the pressure and cook for 2–3 minutes, depending on the thickness of your vegetables, then fast release.

Sprinkle with the sesame seeds and serve immediately.

MISO-ROAST BRUSSELS SPROUTS

Serves 4

1 tbsp olive oil

500g (1lb 2oz) Brussels sprouts, trimmed and halved

15g (½oz) butter

2 tsp miso paste

1 tbsp dark soy sauce

Sea salt and freshly ground black pepper

I can eat roast Brussels any which way, but this is a favourite. The combination of butter and miso ramps up the savoury qualities and is so satisfying that I could quite happily eat a bowl of these on their own, maybe with a sprinkle of chilli flakes added halfway through.

Heat your pressure cooker and add the oil. When hot, add the Brussels sprouts, cut side down. Leave for at least a couple of minutes until they are well browned, then give it a stir. Season with salt and pepper.

Pour in 50ml (1¾fl oz) of water and click the lid into place as soon as you can to trap all the steam created as the water hits the hot base of the cooker. Bring up to high pressure, adjust the heat so it is just high enough to maintain the pressure and cook for 1 minute. Fast release.

Add the butter, miso paste and soy sauce to the cooker and stir the sprouts on a low heat until they are well coated.

ROAST BEETROOT (WITH THEIR GREENS)

Serves 4

1 bunch of beetroot (600g/1lb 5oz)

1 tsp dried oregano

3 tbsp olive oil

3 garlic cloves, sliced

Juice of ½ lemon

Sea salt and freshly ground black pepper

This is the Greek way with beetroot – roast, peeled and served warm with their stems and greens. No vinegar in sight, thank goodness, just garlic and oil.

Separate the beetroot from their leaves by twisting the stems until they break. Pick over the leaves, wash thoroughly and set aside. Put the beetroot in your pressure cooker, sprinkle in half the oregano and add a splash of water in the base – around 100ml (3½fl oz) is plenty. Close the lid and bring up to high pressure. Adjust the heat so it is just high enough to maintain the pressure and cook, depending on the size of the beets – 4 minutes for tiny ones, 10 for the largest. They should be cooked, but firm. Remove from the heat and leave to drop pressure naturally. When cool enough to handle, slip off the skins and slice.

Wash and reheat your cooker. Add 1 tablespoon of the oil. When hot, quickly sauté the garlic and sprinkle in the remaining oregano before adding the beetroot leaves. Close the lid, bring up to high pressure then immediately remove from the heat. Fast release. Remove the leaves and roughly chop.

Pile the beetroot and leaves onto a serving dish and season with salt and pepper. Add the remaining olive oil and a generous squeeze of lemon juice.

SIMPLE
CORNBREAD

Serves 8

150g (5½oz) cornmeal, fine or coarse

½ tsp bicarbonate of soda
(baking soda)

½ tsp salt

225ml (7¾fl oz) buttermilk
(or 200ml (7fl oz) milk with the
juice of 1 small lemon added)

2 eggs, beaten

25g (¾oz) butter

2 tbsp maple syrup (optional)

OPTIONAL EXTRAS

200g (7oz) sweetcorn – kernels whole
or puréed, or a mixture of the two

100g (3½oz) cooked bacon lardons

2 tbsp pickled jalapeños, chopped

100g (3½oz) grated (shredded) hard
cheese, such as Cheddar or Gruyère,
or crumbled feta

This is a really simple version which will take all kinds of additions. I like to put butter and maple syrup on it before I put it under the grill, and then serve with savoury dishes, but you can stud it with corn (recommended), fried bacon, pickled jalapeños, grated cheese or diced feta or queso fresco. In my house it is served with any kind of chilli.

Put the cornmeal in a bowl with the bicarbonate of soda and salt. Mix the buttermilk and eggs together than add to the dry ingredients, keeping mixing to a minimum. Add in any extras.

Melt half the butter in an 18cm (7in) diameter baking tin or ovenproof dish. When it is hot and foaming, quickly add the cornmeal batter then cover the dish with foil. Pour 2cm (¾in) of water into your pressure cooker. Put in a trivet and place the dish on top. Close the lid and bring up to high pressure. Adjust the heat so it is just high enough to maintain the pressure, cook for 20 minutes, then remove from the heat and leave to drop pressure naturally.

Preheat your grill (broiler) to its highest setting. Prick the surface of the cornbread lightly with a skewer then dot the remaining butter on top. Drizzle with the maple syrup if using, then put under a grill – or use an air-fryer lid – for a few minutes until dappled light brown in places. Serve hot, cut into wedges.

A KIND OF DAUPHINOISE

Serves 4-6

30g (1oz) butter, plus extra for greasing

1 garlic clove, finely chopped

750g (1lb 10oz) floury potatoes, unpeeled and thinly sliced

Nutmeg, for grating

1 tsp plain (all-purpose) flour

250ml (9fl oz) whipping (heavy) cream

Sea salt and freshly ground black pepper

OPTIONAL EXTRAS

1 leek, trimmed and finely sliced

50ml (1¾fl oz) white wine or vermouth

100g (3½ oz) grated (shredded) hard cheese

You can make this as the classic or you can include leek and cheese for a change. It is up to you whether or not you brown it under the grill.

First cut a piece of baking paper to fit snugly inside your pressure cooker. Scrunch it lightly, smooth out so it lies flat, then smear with butter. Set aside.

If using the leek, cook it lightly first – this ensures the gratin isn't flooded with liquid. Heat your pressure cooker and add half the butter. When melted, add the leek and stir until coated in butter. Add the wine and season with salt and pepper. Close the lid, bring up to high pressure and immediately remove from the heat. Fast release. Remove the leeks from the cooker (don't discard the buttery pan juices – these can be added to any soups or casseroles) and wipe out the cooker.

Melt the remaining butter in your cooker and add the garlic. Sauté for a minute or two. Remove from the heat and layer the potato and leek slices in your cooker (if using), seasoning with salt and pepper and rasps of nutmeg as you go. Whisk the flour into the cream and pour over the layers. Sprinkle over the cheese, if using.

Lay the baking paper, butter side down, over the gratin. Close the lid and bring up to high pressure. Adjust the heat so it is just high enough to maintain the pressure and cook for 3 minutes, then remove from the heat. Leave to stand for 5 minutes before releasing any remaining pressure. If you want to brown the cheese before serving, wrap the cooker handles in foil and put under a grill (broiler). Alternatively, use an air-fryer lid or a blowtorch.

CORN ON
THE COB

Serves 4

1 tbsp olive oil

4 corn on the cob, husked and
cut in half

Sea salt

FOR THE CHIPOTLE
BUTTER

100g (3½oz) butter, softened

2 tsp chipotle paste

FOR THE TOPPING

100g (3½oz) feta or other
crumbly cheese (cotija if you can
get it) or Cheddar, grated (shredded),
if you prefer

3 spring onions (scallions), finely
chopped

2 limes, zested then cut in wedges,
for squeezing

1 small bunch of coriander (cilantro),
finely chopped

2 tbsp pickled jalapeños, finely
chopped (optional)

You can steam corn on the cob in the pressure cooker incredibly quickly, using much less water than normal. This method gives a little bit of charring, which is entirely optional, but you can skip that step if you just want it steamed. You can also steam this way before putting the cobs on a barbecue - it will save you lots of time.

First prepare the butter and topping. Mash the softened butter with the chipotle paste and plenty of salt. Mix together the topping ingredients. Set aside.

Heat your pressure cooker - or a frying pan (skillet) if you prefer or your cooker has a sensitive burn sensor - and add the oil. When hot, add the corn and sear on one side before flipping. You don't need the whole cobs to be browned; go for a piebald effect. Season with salt.

Add 100ml (3½fl oz) of water and close the lid. Bring up to high pressure and immediately remove from the heat and fast release if your corn is very fresh. If not, cook for 1 minute.

Remove the corn from the cooker. Slather with butter and sprinkle with the toppings. Serve hot.

VARIATION

The cooked corn also makes for great quesadillas. Strip the kernels from the cobs, toss in a tablespoon of the chipotle butter and mix with the topping ingredients, plus 100g (3½oz) of cooked black beans, if you like. Then use to sandwich together tortillas and lightly fry.

COCONUT RICE

Serves 4-6

1 tbsp coconut oil

300g (10½oz) basmati or jasmine rice, well rinsed and drained

150ml (5fl oz) coconut cream

Sea salt and freshly ground black pepper

OPTIONAL EXTRAS

Finely chopped coriander (cilantro)

Lime zest

This is a sweeter, creamier take on rice, particularly good for pairing with a hot and sour curry.

Heat your pressure cooker and add the coconut oil. When melted, add the rice. Stir for a minute or two until the grains are coated then pour in the coconut cream and 450ml (16fl oz) of water. Season with plenty of salt and pepper.

Bring up to high pressure, then adjust the heat so it is just high enough to maintain the pressure. Cook for 3 minutes, then remove from the heat and leave to drop pressure naturally.

Remove the lid and place a folded tea towel or cloth over the top of the cooker. Sit the lid loosely on top and leave, off the heat, to steam for at least 5 minutes, preferably 10. Stir in the coriander or lime zest (or both) and serve.

SESAME RICE

Serves 4-6

15g (½oz) butter

1 tbsp white sesame seeds

1 garlic clove, crushed

300g (10½oz) basmati or jasmine rice, well rinsed and drained

1–2 tbsp soy sauce

2 tsp toasted sesame oil

2 spring onions (scallions), finely chopped

Sea salt

A great accompaniment to all kinds of dishes, this is also good as a base for a salad. If you would prefer to make it with brown rice, increase the cook time to 10 minutes but don't add any extra liquid.

Heat your pressure cooker and add the butter. When melted, add the sesame seeds and toast for a minute or two, then stir in the garlic and rice. Stir in 450ml (16fl oz) of water and season with salt. Steam in the same way as the Coconut Rice, above. Stir in the soy sauce and toasted sesame oil, and serve, garnished with the spring onions.

BROWN RICE AND LENTIL PILAF

Serves 4-6

1 tbsp olive or coconut oil

200g (7oz) brown basmati rice

75g (2½oz) brown or green lentils, rinsed

5g (¼oz) piece of ginger, grated (minced)

2 garlic cloves, crushed or grated (minced)

100g (3½oz) kale leaves, shredded (optional)

Sea salt and freshly ground black pepper

The rice here will have a robust texture – I like it with vegetable-based, coconut curries, such as the one on page 80.

Heat your pressure cooker and add the oil. When hot, add the rice, lentils, ginger, garlic and kale if using. Sauté for a couple of minutes, then season with salt and pepper. Cover with 400ml (14fl oz) of water and close the lid. Bring up to high pressure and adjust the heat so it is just high enough to maintain the pressure. Cook for 8 minutes, then remove from the heat and leave to drop pressure naturally.

BULGAR WHEAT PILAF

Serves 4

1 tbsp olive oil

1 courgette (zucchini), grated (optional)

150g (5½oz) bulgar wheat

½ tsp ground allspice

½ tsp dried mint

Sea salt and freshly ground black pepper

This goes especially well with the Spiced Lamb and Aubergines on page 57.

Heat your pressure cooker and add the oil. When hot, add the courgette (zucchini), if using, and sauté until it has collapsed and is looking dry. Stir in the bulgar wheat, allspice and mint, then add 300ml (10½fl oz) of water. Season with salt and plenty of pepper.

Make sure that all the bulgar wheat is submerged (some grains will need brushing down from the sides), then close the lid. Bring up to high pressure, adjust the heat so it is just high enough to maintain the pressure and cook for 2 minutes. Remove from the heat and leave to drop pressure naturally.

A CHEAT RICE
AND PEAS

Serves 4-6

1 tbsp coconut or olive oil

300g (10½oz) basmati or other
long-grain rice, well rinsed
and drained

A large sprig of thyme

½ tsp ground allspice

250g (9oz) cooked red kidney beans,
black beans or lentils (see page 231 for
cooking instructions)

Sea salt and freshly ground
black pepper

**This is good as a side but I also like it as a plain main course. If I am
not planning on serving it with anything too spicy, I might throw in
a whole Scotch bonnet too.**

Heat your pressure cooker and add the oil. When hot, add the rice
and sauté for a couple of minutes. Add 450ml (16fl oz) of water, then
the thyme, allspice and beans. Season with plenty of salt and pepper.
Bring up to high pressure and adjust the heat so it is just high enough
to maintain the pressure. Cook for 3 minutes, then remove from the
heat and leave to drop pressure naturally.

SWEET THINGS

When I was growing up, my mother used her pressure cooker mainly for sweet things, especially the Christmas pudding, but also a really good lemon and honey sponge. Of course, back in those days I had a much sweeter tooth and preferred the Heinz puddings my grandmother gave me. Now I have my own family and use my pressure cooker every single day – more for savoury than sweet dishes – but I still have a fondness for that kind of steamed pudding.

Most of the dishes in this chapter are of that ilk – homely, nostalgic, some very economical too. But they can all be dressed up to be more elegant. There isn't a single one I wouldn't serve up at a dinner party (Do people still have dinner parties? I am unsure).

I have tried to get the balance right between those which can be cooked very quickly in the main body of the pressure cooker, and those which rely on the 'pot in pot' method, which is essentially treating the pressure cooker like a bain marie. The cooking time of these is nothing compared to how long it takes conventionally, and the texture is way better.

Remember that with pressure cooker cakes and puddings, it is important to steam without pressure to start with. This gives the raising agents a chance to do their job.

THE SIMPLEST OF BAKED CHEESECAKES

Serves 6-8

FOR THE BASE

50g (1¾oz) butter

125g (4½oz) biscuits (cookies), blitzed to a crumb

1 tbsp cocoa

25g (1oz) dark chocolate, grated

FOR THE TOPPING

250g (9oz) cream cheese

250g (9oz) Greek yogurt

397g (14oz) can of condensed milk

1 tbsp strong espresso or coffee extract

1 tbsp Frangelico or other nut or coffee liqueur (optional)

I have made many cheesecakes in the pressure cooker but none quite so simple as this one. It comes from a South Asian-inspired cheesecake which involves a topping of just condensed milk and yogurt. Excellent, but a little sweet for my tastes, so I came up with this one. The texture is perfect – dense, rich – it cuts beautifully and, believe me, a little goes a very long way.

You can make it completely plain – just biscuits and butter in the base, and cream cheese, yogurt and condensed milk in the topping – for a great dessert using only five ingredients. But I can't leave things alone, so have come up with this version.

And why bake? Well, it is all about getting that perfect texture.

Base-line a deep-sided, 18cm (7in) loose-bottomed or springform cake tin with baking paper.

First make the base. Melt the butter in a pan, then remove from the heat and stir in the biscuit crumbs, cocoa and chocolate. Press into the lined tin and refrigerate while you make the topping.

Beat the cream cheese until smooth, then work in the yogurt and condensed milk. Add the coffee a teaspoon at a time, mixing thoroughly and tasting as you go; I find that a tablespoon gives just the right intensity. Stir in the liqueur, if using.

Pour the topping over the biscuit base and give the tin a gentle shake. Lift up the tin a few times and drop onto your work surface – this will help dislodge air bubbles. Cover with foil.

Pour 2cm (¾in) of water into the base of your cooker and add a trivet. Set the cake tin on top. Close the lid and place over a high heat. Bring up to high pressure then adjust the heat until it is just high enough to maintain the pressure. Cook for 25 minutes, then remove from the heat and leave to drop pressure naturally.

Remove the tin from the cooker and leave to cool down completely. For the best texture, refrigerate for a few hours. Serve with crème fraîche if you wish.

LEMON PÔTS DE CRÈME

Serves 4

Butter or oil, for greasing

300ml (10½fl oz) single (light) cream

100g (3½oz) caster (superfine) sugar

Pared zest of 1 lemon

4 egg yolks

So easy, these, and they take so little time to cook that if you want to make more you can cook in batches, no problem. Plus, they will work with any kind of citrus. Try with Seville orange zest in the winter - you won't be disappointed.

Serve on their own, perhaps with a little almond biscuit (cookie) on the side. Oh, and you can booze them up if you like - a tablespoon of limoncello certainly won't hurt.

Lightly butter or oil 4 medium ramekins. Cut rounds of baking paper to fit on top of the ramekins and butter them too.

Put the cream, half the sugar and pared lemon zest in a small saucepan and stir over a low heat until the sugar has dissolved. Remove from the heat and leave to infuse until the mixture is completely cool, but preferably for at least 30 minutes.

Beat the remaining sugar and egg yolks in a large bowl until well combined but not aerated – you don't want any foam. Pour the cream mixture over the eggs and sugar, and gently stir to combine. Strain into a jug, then divide between the ramekins. Try to get rid of any bubbles – you can do this by dropping the ramekins from a short height onto the work surface. Cover with the rounds of baking paper, butter side down.

Pour 2cm (¾fl oz) of water into your pressure cooker and add the trivet and a steamer basket. Place the ramekins in the basket.

Close the lid and place over a high heat. Bring your cooker to high pressure and adjust the heat so it is just high enough to maintain the pressure. Cook for 5 minutes, then fast release. Remove the ramekins and leave to cool completely before transferring to the fridge. Chill thoroughly before serving.

CHOCOLATE AND ALMOND CAKE

Serves 8-10

125g (4½oz) butter, softened, plus extra for greasing

100g (3½oz) caster (superfine) sugar

50g (1¾oz) cocoa

50g (1¾oz) plain (all-purpose) flour

100g (3½oz) ground almonds

1 tsp baking powder

Pinch of salt

3 eggs

50ml (1¾fl oz) crème fraîche or soured cream

50g (1¾oz) dark chocolate, coarsely grated

FOR THE CHOCOLATE SYRUP (OPTIONAL)

100g (3½oz) icing sugar

25g (1oz) cocoa

1-2 tbsp (or to taste) almond liqueur or rum (optional)

This is quite a dense, rich cake which works well warm from the cooker as a dessert as well as cold. If you add the syrup as well it becomes a chocolate drizzle cake. Also, if you want to add alcohol to it and are serving children, you can instead drizzle it over, warm, at the table instead of using it to soak the whole cake.

Grease and base-line a 20cm (8in) cake tin.

Beat the butter and sugar together in a mixing bowl until very soft and aerated. Mix the cocoa, flour, almonds and baking powder together with a pinch of salt. Add the dry mix, the eggs, the crème fraîche or soured cream and the grated chocolate to the butter/sugar mixture and gently fold everything in together.

Spoon into the lined tin and smooth over as much as you can - this batter is quite dense so may be a bit resistant. Cover the tin with foil.

Pour 3cm (1¼in) of water into your pressure cooker and add a trivet. Place the tin on top of the trivet, using a foil sling if it is a tight fit. Loosely cover the cooker with the lid and place over a high heat. As soon as steam starts to appear, time for 15 minutes. Check the water level and top up if necessary then close the lid and bring up to high pressure. Adjust the heat so it is just high enough to maintain the pressure, and cook for 20 minutes. Remove from the heat and leave to drop pressure naturally.

Remove from the pressure cooker but leave the cake in the tin.

If using the syrup, put the sugar and cocoa in a small saucepan and add 100ml (3½fl oz) of water. Whisk to combine and simmer until syrupy. Add the alcohol to taste, if using. Poke holes all over the top of the cake and pour over half the syrup, reserving the rest to add just before serving.

Serve warm or hot, or leave to cool in the tin. Either way, pour over the remaining syrup before serving.

APPLE
SNOW

Serves 4

500g (1lb 2oz) Bramley apples,
peeled, cored and sliced

A squeeze of lemon juice

50g (1¾oz) caster sugar

½ cinnamon stick

1 egg white

FOR THE TOPPING (OPTIONAL)

1 tbsp dark muscovado sugar

¼ tsp ground cinnamon

A pinch of ground allspice

A pinch of ground cloves

TO SERVE

Single (light) cream, for drizzling

Biscuits (cookies) of your choice

I had forgotten how much I like this. I have been making it with apples but also with the glut of quince I had this year (see the variation). We eat as it is with the egg white, or my children stir it through yogurt.

Toss the prepared apples in the lemon juice to help prevent browning. Put 50ml (1¾oz) of water in the base of your pressure cooker and set over a high heat. Add the apples, then sprinkle over the sugar. Add the cinnamon stick. Stir to combine. You should start seeing steam appear. Close the lid and bring up to high pressure. Cook for 2 minutes at high pressure, adjusting the heat so it is just high enough to maintain the pressure then remove from the heat and leave to drop pressure naturally. You should find that the apple slices will have puffed up and even if they still keep their shape (those on top will do so), they will be very soft. Beat with a spoon to a purée – you can push through a coarse sieve if you want it extra-smooth, but it shouldn't be necessary.

Transfer the purée to a bowl or container and leave to cool, then chill in the fridge. When the apples are quite cold, whisk the egg white to the stiff peaks stage. Carefully fold this into the apple mixture, then divide between dessert bowls or glasses.

For the topping, if using, mix the sugar with the spices and sprinkle over the apple snow. The sugar will start to dissolve and add a hint of spiced butterscotch to the apples. Serve with a drizzle of cream and some biscuits for dipping.

VARIATION

Making this with quince produces a beautiful, blush-coloured and fragrant dessert. Increase the cooking time to 3 minutes at high pressure.

CINNAMON AND BAY-SCENTED RICE PUDDING

Serves 4-6

150g (5½oz) pudding or short-grain rice

900ml (31fl oz) whole milk

75g (2½oz) caster (superfine) sugar

40g (1½oz) butter

2 bay leaves

1 strip of pared lemon zest

½ cinnamon stick

This is really good with any of the fruit compôtes on pages 222-23. It makes sense to make the compôte first so you can heat it through when your rice pudding is ready to serve. Or you can chill both – it works really well.

Put all the ingredients in your pressure cooker and stir to make sure nothing is sticking. Close the lid and place over a high heat. Bring up to high pressure. Adjust the heat so it is just high enough to maintain the pressure and cook for 15 minutes. Remove from the heat and leave to drop pressure naturally.

Give the pudding a good stir and leave to stand for a few minutes – it will thicken as it cools. Fish out the bay leaves and cinnamon stick.

Serve hot or cold.

A TRIO OF COMPÔTES

Compôte works really well with rice pudding (see page 219), stirred through yogurt, or simply served with a dollop of cream and a sprinkling of chopped nuts.

DRIED APRICOT COMPÔTE

Serves 4

250g (9oz) dried, pitted apricots

1–2 tbsp runny honey

A generous pinch of saffron

Juice of ½ orange

1 strip of pared lemon zest

A few drops of rose water

I know we are supposed to use the unsulphured apricots, but for desserts such as this, I'm afraid I do want the orange ones. I could make this just for the aroma that fills the kitchen - it is heaven. I serve it with slightly sweetened ricotta or mascarpone and a few flaked almonds or pistachios.

Put the apricots in your pressure cooker. Drizzle over 1 tablespoon of the honey and sprinkle over the saffron. Add the orange juice and lemon zest and pour in 150ml (5fl oz) of water. Heat gently until the honey has dissolved, then close the lid. Bring up to high pressure and adjust the heat so it is just high enough to maintain the pressure. Cook for 5 minutes, then remove from the heat and leave to drop pressure naturally.

Add a few drops of rose water, then taste and add the rest of the honey and more rose water if necessary. Cool before serving.

BLACKBERRY AND APPLE COMPÔTE

Serves 4

500g (1lb 2oz) eating apples (about 3 medium), peeled, cored and cut into wedges

Juice of ½ lemon

10g (¼oz) butter

25g (1oz) caster (superfine) sugar

¼ tsp ground cinnamon (optional)

150g (5½oz) blackberries, preferably frozen

I also like this made with pears and blueberries.

Toss the prepared apples in the lemon juice to help prevent browning. Heat your pressure cooker and add the butter. When melted and starting to foam, add the sugar and cinnamon, if using, and stir until the sugar has dissolved. Add the apples and stir to coat. Throw in the blackberries and 50ml (1¾fl oz) of water. Stir to make sure nothing is sticking.

Close the lid and bring up to high pressure. Remove from the heat immediately and leave to drop pressure naturally. The compôte will thicken as it cools.

PLUM AND ORANGE COMPÔTE

Serves 4

Juice of 2 oranges

2 tbsp golden caster (superfine) sugar

1 tsp vanilla extract

1 tsp ground ginger

½ tsp ground cinnamon

8 firm plums, stoned and quartered

This is a good one to make with those 'home-ripening' plums which you know are never going to be as nice eaten raw as they should be.

Put the juice, sugar, vanilla extract and spices into your pressure cooker and stir over a low heat until the sugar has dissolved. Add the plums, skin side down. Close the lid and bring up to high pressure. Adjust the heat so it is just high enough to maintain the pressure. Cook for 1 minute, then remove from the heat and leave to drop pressure naturally. Give the compôte a stir – you should find the plums have collapsed and will easily stir into a well-textured purée. Taste for sweetness and add more sugar or a drizzle of honey if necessary.

INDIVIDUAL STEAMED PUDDINGS

Makes 8

200g (7oz) butter, softened, plus extra for greasing

200g (7oz) golden caster (superfine) sugar

200g (7oz) self-raising (self-rising) flour

1 tsp baking powder

Pinch of salt

3 eggs

1 tsp vanilla extract

2–3 tbsp milk

Custard (bought or see the Proper Custard on page 227) or cream, to serve

FOR THE TOPPING

8 tablespoons of jam, marmalade, golden syrup or curd

Making individual steamed puddings means you can make a variety of flavours. You can apply the timings and basic quantities to any steamed pudding you like. I might use citrus zest and juice in place of vanilla extract and milk, for example. They also don't take long to cook in these 150ml (5fl oz) basins and freeze really well, perfect for a quick dessert.

Take eight pudding basins and coat the insides with butter. Set aside.

Beat the butter and sugar together in a mixing bowl until well aerated. Whisk the flour and baking powder together with a pinch of salt. Add this to the butter/sugar mixture, along with the eggs, and combine. Add the vanilla and just enough milk to make a dropping consistency.

Put a tablespoon of your choice of topping in the base of each pudding basin. Divide the sponge batter equally between the pudding basins (I'm afraid I weigh them so I can do this very precisely).

Take eight pieces of foil or baking paper and fold a pleat into each one. Secure around the tops of the basins with string or elastic bands.

Set your pressure cooker over a high heat and put a piece of fabric in the base – this is to stop the puddings from jiggling around too much. Arrange the puddings on top of the fabric. Pour water around the basins to come 2–3cm (¾–1in) up the sides. If your cooker is wide, you can cook the puddings in a single layer, otherwise you may have to balance them on top of one another.

As soon as steam starts to appear, put the lid on loosely and allow the puddings to steam for 10 minutes. Then close the lid tightly and bring up to high pressure. Adjust the heat so it is just high enough to maintain the pressure and cook for 15 minutes. Remove from the heat and leave to drop pressure naturally.

Turn the puddings out into individual bowls and serve with the custard or cream. To reheat a pudding from chilled or room temperature, steam as above by just bringing up to high pressure, then remove from the heat immediately and leave to drop pressure naturally. If you are reheating from frozen, cook for 1 minute at high pressure and leave to drop pressure naturally.

PEACH AND BLUEBERRY BREAD PUDDING

Serves 4

50g (1¾oz) melted butter, plus extra for greasing and to finish

250g (9oz) bread (any sort), torn

1 tsp baking powder

75g (2½oz) soft light brown sugar

½ tsp ground cinnamon

250ml (9fl oz) whole milk

1 egg

1 tsp vanilla extract

2 peaches, cut into wedges, or canned equivalent

100g (1½oz) blueberries

2 tbsp demerara sugar (raw brown sugar)

Custard (bought or see the Proper Custard, opposite) or cream, to serve

The combination of peaches and blueberry is one of my favourites. It is also a useful one because you can get away with using canned peaches and frozen blueberries, making this good in an emergency (yes, we all have emergency dessert situations). The best cobbler I ever had was definitely made with canned peaches. In syrup!

Butter and line an 18–20cm (7–8in) cake tin or ovenproof dish. Put the bread in a mixing bowl and add the baking powder, sugar and cinnamon. Whisk the milk, egg, vanilla and melted butter together and pour over the bread mixture. Mix thoroughly, breaking up the pieces as much as you can – this is easiest done with your hands.

Stir in the peaches and blueberries. Pile everything into the prepared tin and press down firmly. Cover with foil.

Pour 2cm (¾in) of water into your pressure cooker. Add a trivet and place the tin on top, using a foil sling if necessary. Close the lid and place over a high heat. Bring up to high pressure and adjust the heat so it is just high enough to maintain the pressure. Cook for 30 minutes, then remove from the heat and leave to drop pressure naturally.

Dot the pudding with butter and sprinkle with demerara sugar. Put under a preheated grill (broiler) for a couple of minutes, just to crisp it up.

Serve hot with custard or cream.

PROPER
CUSTARD

Serves 4-6

4 egg yolks

2 tbsp caster (superfine) sugar

300ml (10½fl oz) whole milk

1 tsp vanilla extract

1 coffee bean (optional)

The coffee bean isn't essential here, but it is amazing how much it improves the flavour, without making your custard taste of coffee! Don't worry if your custard doesn't look smooth when you open your pressure cooker – it will soon come together when you whisk it.

Pour 2cm (¾in) of water into your pressure cooker. Put in either a folded cloth or the trivet.

Put the egg yolks and sugar in a bowl small enough to fit inside your cooker and stir to combine. Stir in the milk, vanilla and coffee bean, if using. Cover with baking paper.

Place the bowl on the cloth or trivet, using a foil sling if necessary. Close the lid and bring up to high pressure. Adjust the heat so it is just high enough to maintain the pressure and cook for 5 minutes, then fast release. Whisk briefly to create a smooth texture – the custard will thicken as it cools.

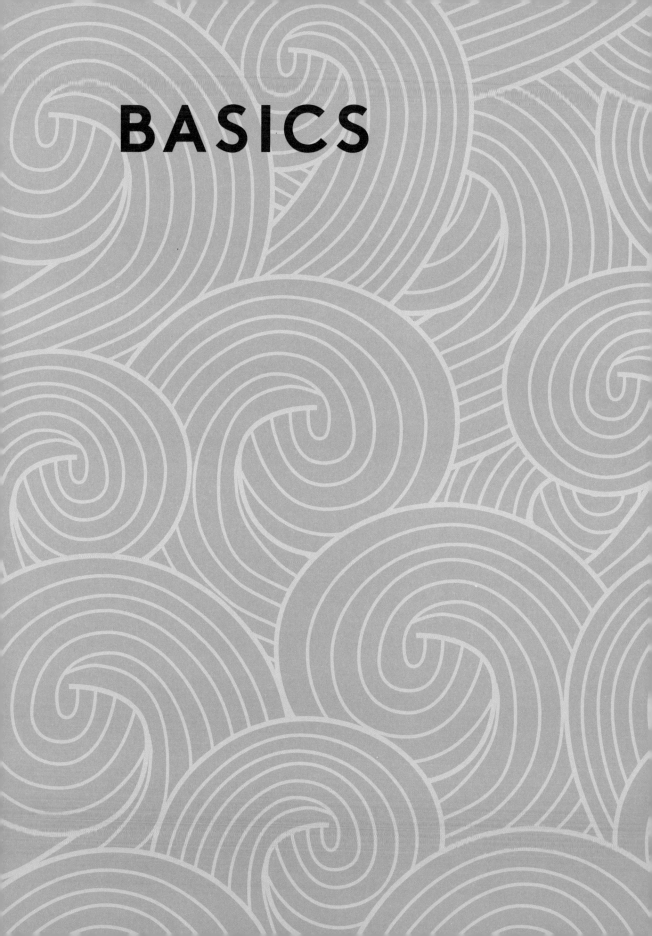

BASICS

This chapter contains a few simple basic recipes, how-tos and hacks to help you make the most of your pressure cooker, especially if you have a freezer and/or you like batch cooking. I hope that at least some of them will be a boon – they certainly make my life much easier.

If you plan to batch cook, I would recommend freezing in various amounts, or in the case of beans, pulses and grains, ensure that you open-freeze them first so that they are stored loose (like a bag of peas or sweetcorn), then you can measure out what you need. Any blocks of frozen foods can be defrosted really easily. All I do is put a splash of water in the pressure cooker, drop in the frozen food, bring up to high pressure, immediately remove from the heat and leave to drop pressure naturally.

COOKING BEANS

Most recipes in this book use cooked beans as that is what most people prefer to use when they are in a hurry to get dinner on the table. I have kept the quantities to roughly the equivalent of drained cans, as I know it is likely most people will depend on these at some point. But if you cook your own and either keep in the fridge for up to a week or freeze in handy 250g (9oz) portions for when you need them, you will save yourself a small fortune.

THERE ARE SEVERAL WAYS TO COOK BEANS

From dry or unsoaked. This is good if you are in a hurry, but bad in terms of fuel cost as it takes much longer. Also, texture-wise, the beans are not quite as good.

From soaked, using either of these methods:

Traditional soaking
Cover the dried beans in cold water and add 1 teaspoon of salt. Leave overnight, then drain.

Quick soaking
Put the dried beans in your pressure cooker, cover with cold water and add 1 teaspoon of salt and 1 tablespoon of oil. Bring up to high pressure, adjust the heat so it is just high enough to maintain the pressure, and cook for 2 minutes. Remove from the heat and leave to stand for 5 minutes. Release any remaining pressure and drain.

TO COOK

Put the beans in your pressure cooker and add cold water to cover by at least 2cm (¾in), 1 teaspoon of salt and 1 tablespoon each of oil and any kind of vinegar. You can add any aromatics at this point. Make sure you don't fill over the two-thirds mark. Bring up to high pressure and cook for the times set out opposite. Remove from the heat and leave to drop pressure naturally before straining as soon as the pressure has dropped (otherwise they will overcook).

Lentils do not generally need soaking – the exception being urud dal.

TIMINGS

As pressure cookers cook at different temperatures, and because beans vary enormously in how they cook due to age, etc, there are two timings for these. Go with the lower the first time you cook them – it is always better to undercook than overcook.

Type	Mins cooking (unsoaked)	Mins cooking (soaked)
Black beans	22–25	4–6
Black-eyed peas	6–9	3–5
Borlotti (Cranberry)	19–22	7–10
Butter (Lima), Gigantes	12–15	5–7
Cannellini beans/Calypso (Orca, Yin Yang)	25–30	5–8
Chickpeas (Garbanzo beans)/ Carlin peas/Badger	28–35	13–20
Fava (dried broad bean)	25–30	10
Flageolet	18–25	6–8
Gungo/Pigeon peas (whole)	25	12–15
Haricot (navy) beans	18–25	6–8
Kidney (red) beans	25–30	6–8
Marrowfat peas	20	6–8
Mung beans	7	
Pinto beans	19–22	7–10
Soya beans	28–35	20
Black beluga lentils	6	
Channa dal (split chickpeas)	2–3 (2 to keep shape, 3 to break down)	
Green/brown/Puy lentils	1–2 minutes for al dente	
Red lentils/split peas	1–2 minutes (1 to keep shape, 2 to break down)	
Urud dal (white, split)	5	
Urud dal (white, whole)	12	5

COOKING GRAINS (AND SHORT PASTA)

There are lots of examples of how to cook grains throughout the book, but here are some basic rules, timings and grain-to-liquid ratios. This is important because grains are usually cooked by the absorption method (using just the right amount of liquid to cook the grain).

Rinse the grains – most need some starch removing, all (except short-grain rice) benefit from washing. Drain thoroughly.

Toast – this is generally to improve flavour but also reduces starch build-up and sticking. Simply heat your pressure cooker, add oil and, when hot, toast the grain until any liquid has steamed off and it is giving off a nutty aroma.

Add the right amount of liquid (water, stock, etc) and aromatics.

Bring up to high pressure and cook according to the timings opposite. Drop pressure naturally. As an option, you can leave to steam, off the heat, to fluff up any grain or long-grain rice by placing a tea towel or cloth over the cooker and loosely covering with the lid. Leave for 10 minutes.

Type	Ratio grain:liquid	Cook at high pressure
Barley (pearled)	1:2	18 minutes
Buckwheat groats	1:1	3 minutes
Bulgar wheat	1:1 minute (al dente), 2 minutes (softer)	
Farro	1: 2.5	10 minutes
Freekeh	1:2	10 minutes
Giant couscous	1: 2.5	1 minute
Millet	1:3	1 minute
Quinoa	1:2	1 minute
Spelt	1:3	12 minutes
White long-grain rice	1: 1.5	3 minutes
Brown/wild/black long-grain rice	1:1.5	18 minutes
Medium grain (sushi, baldo, sticky/glutinous)	1: 1.25	5–6 minutes
Short-grain (risotto) rice (don't rinse)	1: 2.5	5–7 minutes
Brown short-grain rice (don't rinse)	1:2.5	20 minutes

A COUPLE OF QUICK STOCKS

I find you can pretty much manage with just chicken and vegetable stock in any kitchen so these are the ones I try to have on hand.

QUICK CHICKEN STOCK

1–2 chicken carcasses, raw or cooked

2 chicken wings, raw (optional)

1 onion, roughly chopped

1 carrot, roughly chopped

1 celery stick

A few garlic cloves

A few sprigs of herbs (I usually use bay, thyme and tarragon)

1 tsp peppercorns

Put everything in your pressure cooker and cover with 1 litre (35fl oz) cold water. Close the lid and bring to high pressure. Adjust the heat so it is just high enough to maintain the pressure and cook for 30 minutes if using cooked carcasses, or 45 minutes if using raw. Remove from the heat and leave to drop pressure naturally. Strain through a sieve and discard the solids. Once the stock is cool, skim off any fat and store separately if you like. Store the stock in the fridge for up to a week or in the freezer for 3 months.

QUICK VEGETABLE STOCK

This is easiest if you keep a bag of trimmings in your freezer - making sure they are clean and blemish free, of course. Use any vegetables you like apart from starchy potatoes/ground provisions or cruciferous ones. Do include peelings, fibres and rind from pumpkins and squash, pods, trimmings from mushrooms and asparagus, tomato and garlic skins. To make, use roughly double the amount of liquid to solids. Follow the method for the quick chicken stock but cook for just 5 minutes. Leave to cool before straining. Store the stock in the fridge for up to a week or in the freezer for 3 months.

A QUICK SOFFRITTO

Makes 250g (9oz)

50ml (1¾fl oz) olive oil

2 large onions, finely chopped

3 carrots, finely diced

3 celery sticks, finely diced

4 garlic cloves, crushed or grated

Any herbs you like

1 tsp salt

You can use this in any recipes that call for the sautéed onion/carrot/celery combination as the first step – and also those which just have onions too; it will never hurt. A couple of cubes will be enough.

Heat your pressure cooker and add the oil. When hot, add all the remaining ingredients. Stir until the vegetable are hot enough to start creating steam, then close the lid and bring up to high pressure. Adjust the heat so it is just high enough to maintain the pressure and cook for 5 minutes and fast release. Simmer off any excess liquid for a couple of minutes. Store in the fridge for up to a week or freeze in ice-cube trays until frozen, then decant into a freezer-proof bag or container. The cubes can be used straight from frozen.

QUICK PRESERVED
LEMONS

Makes 1 small ½lb jar of preserved lemon - around 200ml

4 lemons

1 tsp sea salt

Preserved lemons are usually either expensive to buy, often with a slight whiff of mustiness about them, or take at least 6 weeks to cure when homemade. This version is instant so can be used immediately, and will also keep indefinitely in the fridge if stored in a sterilized jar. The syrupy lemon juice the zest sits in is very useful in all kinds of ways, including salad dressings. This method also works very well with other types of citrus fruit - try with Seville or blood oranges when they are in season.

Pare the zest off the lemons in thick strips, then scrape off any thick pieces of pith from the zest. Put into the pressure cooker, then juice the lemons and add the juice to the cooker along with the salt. Bring up to high pressure and cook for 2 minutes, then leave to drop pressure naturally.

Transfer to a sterilized jar and cool. Store in the fridge indefinitely.

A FEW SPICY SHORTCUTS

ONION, GARLIC AND GINGER PASTE

Makes 300g (10½oz)

1 tbsp olive or coconut oil

4 large onions, finely sliced

Cloves from 2 heads of garlic

100g (3½oz) piece of ginger, roughly chopped

Sea salt

This is useful if you make a lot of curries; I keep cubes in my freezer. You only need a couple of cubes per curry – here you are concentrating the flavour by removing the excess water from the onions, and especially so if you freeze it.

Heat your pressure cooker and add the oil. When hot, add the onion and salt. Stir until the cooker is giving off plenty of steam. Don't add any extra water – close the lid and bring up to high pressure. Adjust the heat so it is just high enough to maintain the pressure and cook for 3 minutes and fast release. Strain off all the liquid in the cooker (you can use this in soups and stocks).

Put the onion, garlic and ginger in a food processor and blitz to a paste. Store in the fridge or freeze in an ice-cube tray and decant. The cubes can be used straight from frozen.

A FEW SPICE BLENDS

The basic spice mix is my general-purpose curry powder which I use as a base for a lot of my curries. For all these spice blends you can freshly grind your own spices, if you like – toast the whole spices first before grinding and measuring out the quantities. Simply mix the ground spices and store in a sealed jar.

BASIC SPICE MIX

Makes about 50g (1¾oz)

2 tbsp ground cumin

2 tbsp ground coriander

2 tbsp Kashmiri chilli powder

1 tbsp ground turmeric

2 tsp ground fenugreek

1 tsp ground cinnamon

½ tsp ground cloves

OPTIONAL EXTRAS

If I am making a Caribbean-style curry, I will add to the above:

1 tsp ground allspice

AND IF I AM MAKING A VERY SWEET FRAGRANT CURRY I WILL ADD

1 tsp ground allspice

1 tsp ground green cardamom

MEXICAN-STYLE SPICE MIX

Makes about 50g (1¾oz)

Try this multipurpose spice mix for making a chilli or a filling for tortillas.

1 tbsp ground cumin

1 tbsp ground coriander

1 tbsp ground cinnamon

1 tbsp dried oregano

2 tsp garlic powder

2 tsp ground allspice

¼ tsp ground cloves

NORTH AFRICAN-STYLE SPICE MIX

Makes about 50g (1¾oz)

This is the spice mix I use in tagines and other North African dishes.

1 tbsp ground cinnamon

1 tbsp ground cumin

1 tbsp ground coriander

1 tbsp ground ginger

2 tsp ground allspice

2 tsp ground white peppercorns

2 tsp ground cardamom

1 tsp cayenne or hot paprika

1 tsp ground turmeric

¼ tsp ground cloves

BASIC THAI-STYLE CURRY PASTE

These are my everyday curry pastes which are very easy to make and store very well in the freezer. They are based on the idea of Thai curry pastes, but I have found they make useful starting points for all kinds of curries, so I do change them up quite a lot, especially in the type of chillies I use. So do experiment!

RED CURRY PASTE

Makes about 100g (3½oz)

2 shallots or 1 red onion

2 lemongrass stalks, white parts only

10g (¼oz) piece of ginger, sliced

10g (¼oz) galangal, sliced (optional)

6 garlic cloves, sliced

4 red chillies, roughly chopped

2 tbsp finely chopped coriander (cilantro) stems

Zest and juice of 1 lime

1 tsp ground coriander

1 tsp ground turmeric

½ tsp ground cinnamon

Simply put everything in a food processor and pulse until it forms a rough paste – you don't want it completely smooth. You will need to stop and scrape down the sides a couple of times – if it is not combining, a splash of water will help. Store for up to a week in a sealed tub in the refrigerator or freeze in a tub or in an ice-cube tray.

A GENERIC GREEN CURRY PASTE

Makes about 100g (3½oz)

6 green chillies (heat up to you!)

6 garlic cloves

10g ginger

3 lemongrass stalks

2 shallots

1 small bunch coriander

Zest and juice of 1 lime

1 tsp ground white pepper

1 tsp ground coriander

1 tsp ground cumin

½ tsp turmeric

OPTIONAL EXTRAS (TO MAKE IT MORE THAI IN FLAVOUR)

Zest of 1 makrut lime OR 6 lime leaves

1 tsp shrimp paste

10g galangal

A USEFUL
CURRY SAUCE

Makes enough for 2 curries to serve 4

1 tbsp coconut or olive oil

2 large onions, finely chopped

½ head of garlic, cloves finely chopped or grated (minced)

25g (1oz) piece of ginger, finely grated (minced)

2 tbsp your favourite curry powder or use the basic spice mix (see page 241)

2 tsp Kashmiri chilli powder

100g (3½oz) red lentils, well rinsed

400g (14oz) canned tomatoes or coconut milk

1 tbsp tamarind paste (optional)

½ tsp caster (superfine) sugar or honey

250ml (9fl oz) chicken or vegetable stock

Sea salt and freshly ground black pepper

If you batch cook this, you can use it with any meat or vegetables you like, or add in small quantities to rice and soup dishes. I use this a lot, and ring the changes to my curries by frying off whole spices and/or curry leaves at the beginning of the process. I add coriander separately too. Oh, and of course you can use a couple of cubes of the Onion, Garlic and Ginger Paste (page 240) in place of the fresh ingredients here.

Heat your pressure cooker and add the oil. When hot, add the onion and sauté for a few minutes over a medium heat, then add the garlic and ginger. Cook for another couple of minutes, then stir in the spices and red lentils. Pour in the tomatoes or coconut milk and stir in the tamarind paste if using. Sprinkle in the sugar and season with salt and pepper.

Pour in the stock and stir to make sure the base is completely deglazed. Bring up to high pressure then adjust the heat until it is just high enough to maintain the pressure. Cook for 5 minutes. Remove from the heat and leave to drop pressure naturally. Simmer for a few minutes to thicken, then cool before decanting into tubs to store for up to a week in the refrigerator or to freeze.

A FEW VERY USEFUL THINGS I USE MY PRESSURE COOKER FOR...

SOFTENING TOUGH VEGETABLES FOR EASY PREPPING

There are many people who struggle to peel or cut up certain vegetables – I'm thinking tough-skinned squash and pumpkins, swedes, even celeriac (celery root). I find that a blast in the pressure cooker can make a world of difference. I pressure cook unpeeled swede and celeriac for just 5 minutes – this is enough to penetrate the skin and make them softer to peel and dice – and then use them in recipes. A whole pumpkin, though, will usually take 10 minutes to soften enough. Simply put water in your pressure cooker, place the vegetable on a trivet and cook at high pressure. Remove from the heat and leave to drop pressure naturally.

COOKING DUMPLINGS

Whether shop-bought or homemade, you can quickly and easily steam dumplings from frozen or chilled in the pressure cooker; I often find I can do 3–4 batches in the time it takes to do one conventionally. The first batch will take the longest if the water is cold; after that, they will come up to pressure much faster. Pour 2cm (¾in) of water into your cooker, and put the dumplings in a steamer basket. If cooking from frozen, uncooked dumplings will need 3 minutes (high pressure, fast release) or from unfrozen, just 1 minute. If already cooked, dumplings just need heating through, bring up to high pressure, immediately remove from the heat and leave to drop pressure naturally.

REFRESHING STALE BREAD

You may know the trick for quickly running a rock-hard loaf under the cold tap and putting it in the oven. Well, this is the pressure cooker version. Pour 1cm (½in) of water into your cooker. Line the base of a steamer basket with foil (to prevent soggy-bottom bread) and place your bread on top. Bring up to high pressure and fast release. This will give you bread soft enough to slice for toasting or using in dishes such as Panzanella (see page 107) or Bread Pudding (page 226).

MAKING DULCE DE LECHE

Take a can of condensed milk. Pour 1cm (½in) of water into your cooker. Put the unopened can on a folded cloth, either in the base or in a steamer basket. Close the lid and bring up to high pressure. Adjust the heat so it is just high enough to maintain the pressure and cook for 20 minutes for a light caramel, up to 30 for a darker colour. Remove from the heat and leave to drop pressure naturally. Allow to cool before opening the can.

SOFTENING DRIED FRUIT

If you want plump, soft fruit ready to be added to cakes and puddings, here is an instant method. Simply cover dried fruit with an equal weight of liquid – anything you like – and bring up to high pressure. Remove from the heat and leave to drop pressure naturally. You will find that the fruit will have absorbed just about all the liquid.

INDEX

ACKNOWLEDGEMENTS

First of all, thank you to publisher Sarah Lavelle for sticking with me all this time and always believing I have more to write about – this is our sixth book together! And to everyone else at Quadrille, especially Sofie Shearman, who pulled everything together brilliantly and who is responsible for many subtle tweaks which have made the book so much better. Thank you to Katy Everett for giving the book such a fresh and inviting look. And immense gratitude to Stephanie Evans for making sure she understood the pressure cooking process and so was able to provide such thoughtful copyediting.

Thanks to the lovely photoshoot team: Andrew Hayes-Watkins for the best eye and the knack of creating exactly the right atmosphere. Food stylist Mima Sinclair and assistants Georgia Rudd and Marie Guerevich for their ability to make food look good in a way I can only dream of. You are all a joy to work with.

Thank you to all my dear food/writer friends who help me let off steam (pun totally intended), offer the best advice when it is solicited (and sometimes when it's not) and generally help ease the solitary existence of a working-from-home food writer. These especially include Jenny Linford, Jinny Johnson, Mark Diacono, Deborah Robertson, Thane Price, Julia Leonard, Mel Jappy, Fiona Kirkpatrick, Lucy Fisher, Hattie Ellis, Rosie Sykes, Nic Miller, Linda Duffin, Jane Steward, Sue Quinn.

Thank you to everyone who helped promote *Modern Pressure Cooking*, especially Si King, Jay Rayner, India Knight, George Egg, Stefano Arturi, Carla Tomasi, Jenny Chandler, Annie Gray, Bee Wilson and Mallika Basu – you've all shouted out about pressure cooking in general and my work in particular and it never goes unnoticed.

There are too many of you to list here individually but most heartfelt thanks to everyone who has taken the time to message me, asked a question, told me or posted about what they are cooking, followed me to Substack, arranged or attended a demo (often with written lists of questions!). To hear 'life changing' from so many of you has been the best, most gratifying thing. All I want is to know that people are cooking from my books and that it is making life better and easier for them. And just so you all know: every comment and question helps me to decide what I write about next, or sends me down a rabbit hole of exploration and experimentation – you all inform my work in the best of ways.

Thanks to my Hanwell focus group – always helpful, always illuminating: Sandy, Jane x2, Ann-Marie, Kathy, Steven (also responsible for my headshot, thank you for that too, Steven), Jo, Anna, Pamela and most of all Anne Woodgate, who gives great notes.

Thank you to the sage Clare Hulton, agent now for almost 15 years, who is always, always right. I could not manage without you, Clare.

And finally to all my family; Adam and Lilly for providing hands and for eschewing canteen fast food in favour of daily Thermos flasks. To all of you for understanding that our meals are geared around the endless merry-go-round of recipe development and eating it all without complaint (well, apart from Adam who gives me notes. Usually constructive notes). As always, I love you all.

ABOUT THE AUTHOR

Catherine Phipps is a food writer, cookbook author and recipe developer who has frequently featured on TV and radio, including BBC Radio 4's *The Food Programme*. Her previous books include *The Pressure Cooker Cookbook* (2012), *Citrus* (2017), *Leaf* (2019) and *Modern Pressure Cooking* (2022).

Managing Director: Sarah Lavelle
Project Editor: Sofie Shearman
Designer: Katy Everett
Photographer: Andrew Hayes-Watkins
Headshot Photographer: Steven Morris
Food Stylist: Mima Sinclair
Food Stylist Assistants: Georgia Rudd
and Maria Guerevich
Prop Stylist: Rebecca Newport
Head of Production: Stephen Lang
Production Controller: Martina Georgieva

Published in 2024 by Quadrille Publishing Ltd

Quadrille
52–54 Southwark Street
London SE1 1UN
quadrille.com

Cataloguing in Publication Data:
a catalogue record for this book is
available from the British Library.

ISBN 978 1 83783 1760

Printed in China